What God Can Do With An Idiot

What God Can Do With An Idiot

MARK DUTTON, D.Min.

WESTBOW
PRESS®
A DIVISION OF THOMAS NELSON
& ZONDERVAN

Copyright © 2015, 2016 Mark Dutton, D.Min..

All rights reserved. No part of this book may be used or reproduced by any means, graphic, electronic, or mechanical, including photocopying, recording, taping or by any information storage retrieval system without the written permission of the author except in the case of brief quotations embodied in critical articles and reviews.

WestBow Press books may be ordered through booksellers or by contacting:

WestBow Press
A Division of Thomas Nelson & Zondervan
1663 Liberty Drive
Bloomington, IN 47403
www.westbowpress.com
1 (866) 928-1240

Because of the dynamic nature of the Internet, any web addresses or links contained in this book may have changed since publication and may no longer be valid. The views expressed in this work are solely those of the author and do not necessarily reflect the views of the publisher, and the publisher hereby disclaims any responsibility for them.

Any people depicted in stock imagery provided by Thinkstock are models, and such images are being used for illustrative purposes only.
Certain stock imagery © Thinkstock.

All verses are from the NASB unless otherwise noted.

Scripture quotations taken from the New American Standard Bible®, Copyright © 1960, 1962, 1963, 1968, 1971, 1972, 1973, 1975, 1977, 1995 by The Lockman Foundation. Used by permission. (www.Lockman.org)

Scripture taken from the King James Version of the Bible.

ISBN: 978-1-5127-2839-2 (sc)
ISBN: 978-1-5127-2840-8 (hc)
ISBN: 978-1-5127-2841-5 (e)

Library of Congress Control Number: 2016901830

Print information available on the last page.

WestBow Press rev. date: 2/22/2016

CONTENTS

Preface vii

CHAPTER 1	Sin Is Never Logical	1
CHAPTER 2	Adam: The First Human Idiot	8
CHAPTER 3	Noah: Found Favor in the Eyes of the LORD	12
CHAPTER 4	Abraham: A Friend of God	16
CHAPTER 5	Moses: Drawn from the Water	23
CHAPTER 6	Elijah: A Prophet of God	28
CHAPTER 7	Samson: The Strongest Man Who Ever Lived	34
CHAPTER 8	David: A Man After God's Own Heart	40
CHAPTER 9	Rahab: The Harlot	48
CHAPTER 10	Solomon: A Wise Man	52
CHAPTER 11	Jonah: The Word of the Lord Came to Him	59
CHAPTER 12	John: The Disciple Whom Jesus Loved	65
CHAPTER 13	Peter: The Rock	71
CHAPTER 14	Paul: From Saul to Paul	84
CHAPTER 15	We're All Idiots!	107

PREFACE

The title of this book is intended to encourage all of us! The title for each chapter is what it is because I don't want anybody thinking I'm maliciously calling these individuals an idiot. None of us should ever think we can "judge" the life of a person and condemn them by pointing out all of his or her sinful thinking and sinful actions. Instead, I want to communicate the truth from God's Word that sometimes ALL of us think and act in a "stupid" manner because none of us are perfect in our thinking or actions.

In spite of these individuals being an "idiot" for a period of time or a specific moment, God's Word reveals the truth that God's love, grace, mercy, sovereignty, patience, faithfulness, forgiveness, and other attributes allowed Him to use these individuals to impact the lives of others. But most importantly, these people were used to bring glory to God which means to give the right opinion of God. As you will see, that's exactly what happened in spite of the 'stupid choices' each person made.

It's encouraging to know the truth that God has a plan for each one of us. One of the passages in God's Word that has encouraged me in many ways is Jeremiah 29:11-14a: "'For I know the plans that I have for you,' declares the LORD, 'plans for welfare and not for calamity to give you a future and a hope. Then you will call upon Me and come and pray to Me, and I will listen to you. You will seek Me and find Me when you search for me with all your heart. I will be found by you,' declares the Lord."

When we search for God with all of our hearts, we will follow the words of Jesus in Matthew 7:5: "You hypocrite, first take the log out of your own eye, and then you will see clearly to take the speck out of your brother's eye." So as your brother in Christ, or as a friend, I want to encourage you, if you are married, do NOT give this book to your spouse on their birthday or for Christmas; or, as a son or daughter, do NOT give this book to your dad or mom on their birthday or for Christmas. If you do, you're a "stupid idiot"!

CHAPTER 1

Sin Is Never Logical

Many of us—probably almost all of us—were asked some questions by our parents, a brother or sister, a person of authority in our life, our spouse, our children, a fellow believer or even an unbeliever, or a good friend. The questions fell along these lines: Why did you do what you just did? Why didn't you do what you were supposed to do? What were you thinking when you did that? What were you trying to accomplish by your actions? All those questions and many others are good questions because they fit the statement many of us have heard: A question convicts the conscience, but an accusation hardens the heart. A good question tends to make a person think before he or she responds, and it puts the person asking the question in a better position. The one asking the question is not making a judgmental statement by accusing someone of doing something wrong or sinful, especially when the person asking the question doesn't have all the facts or details. Proverbs 18:13 clearly states, "He who gives an answer before he hears, it is folly and shame to him."

Throughout the Bible, God asks a lot of questions to reveal what's taking place in a person's mind or heart. For example, God asked Adam, "Adam, where are you?" and "Have you eaten of the tree that I commanded you not to eat?" Jesus asked the disciples in the New Testament, "Who do you say that I am?" The problem is that the answers we typically give are given to defend our thinking and actions. Instead, we should come right out and admit we were not thinking right, and what was going on in our hearts was the bridge to our sinful actions that were not pleasing to God and did not demonstrate the mind of Christ or the actions that Christ would have taken if He were to face the same situation. Hebrews 4:15 clearly states, "For we do not have a high priest who cannot sympathize with our weaknesses, but One who has been tempted in all things as we are, yet without sin."

Jesus knows exactly what it's like to be tempted to do something sinful, selfish, and stupid. But because Jesus was thinking right, He chose to do right, and all of His thinking and actions gave the right opinion of God. Jesus gave us an example of true holiness in the way we should think and act. If a person doesn't *think* right then that person will not *act* right. That person will make selfish, sinful, and stupid decisions that do not glorify God and will bring hardship and destruction to his or her life, marriage, family, friendships, ministry, relationship to co-workers, neighbors, and many other areas surrounding that person's life.

As I've heard before and stated many times in various lectures and sermons, "Choices have consequences!" The tragedy is not only what happens right now, but also the impact a sinful choice can have on a person's future and the future of the people surrounding that person. Part of the reason for any stupid choice we make is we don't stop and think about the consequences of that stupid choice. Rationalizing that the choice is not wrong can lead us to thinking it's not stupid; therefore, the choice won't hurt or offend anybody. But in reality, it is stupid to sin because we are rejecting the truth of God's Word which has many commands, warnings, and promises for us to follow. We rationalize and justify our sinful thinking and actions, and we don't deal with the reality that sin is never logical. We need to be honest and admit that sin is stupid, ungodly, destructive, and makes no sense compared to the holiness of God or the perfect example Jesus displayed while He was on this earth as a man (John 1:14). Jesus was holy and righteous in the sight of God, and He set an example that we should walk in His steps.

If we allow the light of God's Word to shine on our hearts, we will clearly acknowledge that sin is stupid, selfish, wicked, unholy, condemning, divisive, destructive, and ungodly. It does not bring glory to God, and it's not like Jesus Christ who "also loved you and gave Himself up for us" (Ephesians 5:2). One of the major areas we tend to minimize or often ignore is that sin *always* has a price to be paid. Ezekiel 18:4 clearly warns us, "The soul who sins will die," and Proverbs 13:15 (KJV) says, "But the way of transgressors is hard." Galatians 6:8 tells us, "For the one who sows to his own flesh will from the flesh reap corruption, but the one who sows to the Spirit will from the Spirit reap eternal life."

But thank God, through Jesus Christ and His shed blood, we can be forgiven and have a new life in Christ, and we will live with God for eternity, and the curse of sin will be removed! Once again, Paul made it clear to us as children of God in Galatians 6:8 "For the one who sows to his own flesh will from the flesh reap corruption, but the one who sows to the Spirit will from the Spirit reap eternal life." Even though God has warned us many times throughout His Word about the consequences of sin, we still make stupid choices to disobey God's Word and bring about the results and consequences of our selfish choices which are a result of our selfish thinking because as a man "thinks within himself, so is he" (Proverbs 23:7). Let's admit it: Sinning is stupid! It's not logical, and if we are going to please God, we need to repent which literally means 'a change of the mind.' We also need to obey 1 John 1:9 "If we confess our sins, He is faithful and righteous to forgive us our sins and to cleanse us from all unrighteousness." Confess means to say the same thing God would say. We need to confess our sin to God and to the appropriate people whom we've sinned against. We also need to ask God's forgiveness for the times we are stupid by allowing our sinful thinking to lead to sinful actions instead of allowing our thinking and actions to be controlled by the truth of His Word. We also need to ask forgiveness of the person(s) we have offended, and we need to restore our relationship with God and the person(s) we have offended. And when we are tempted to sin in the future or simply living our daily lives, we should always put on the mind of Christ and make a conscious choice to live like Jesus in the various situations God allows to come into our lives, our marriages, our families, our friendships, our ministries, or any situation.

I remember a friend of mine made a statement that I've never forgotten, but I ignore it when I choose to sin instead of obeying God's Word. The statement was, "There are just two choices on the shelf: pleasing God or pleasing self." Why would a person want to please himself or herself instead of pleasing God who loves us, gave His Son for us to die on the cross to pay the penalty of our sin and rose from the grave three days later to offer us eternal life, and has a place in heaven reserved for us when Jesus returns to take us home to heaven where we will live for eternity? Each one of us has a choice to make every day in every situation, and each one of us can ask this important question: Am I going to please God, or am I going to please myself? If we are smart and godly, we will please God, and if we are stupid and ungodly, we will please ourselves.

A bigger and more important question that truly reveals our heart is, "Why would I sin and want to please myself instead of God?" An honest answer for all of us is that sometimes we think we are smarter than God, and we know what's best for our lives. We think our sincerity about a situation justifies our behavior, no matter what God's Word says about what we are thinking or what we are doing. Sometimes we think that way because God blesses us in many ways, so we think we are right in *every* way. But we all know that is not true because no human being is always right, and if we think we are, we just proved the point that we are not always right! Even though our sins have been paid for on the cross by the blood

SIN IS NEVER LOGICAL

of Christ and we are redeemed, we are still not perfect. In fact, sometimes we are idiots! We all need to admit our need to "grow in grace and in the knowledge of our Lord and Savior, Jesus Christ" (2 Peter 3:18 KJV). We need to get our eyes off of ourselves and what we want, and we should consistently be "looking unto Jesus, the author and finisher of our faith" (Hebrews 12:2 KJV).

However, in all honesty, thinking and acting like we want to please ourselves instead of God is not only illogical; it's stupid and unbiblical, and if we think that way, we are idiots on steroids! If that's the case, then we need to be smart instead of stupid, and we need to be humble instead of proud, and we need to admit our sin of pride and self-righteousness. As Paul wrote in Ephesians 4:22-24, we need to "lay aside the old self" and "be renewed in the spirit of your mind" and "put on the new self which in the likeness of God has been created in righteousness and holiness of the truth." You might be wondering how you can do that. The best way is to stand at the foot of the cross and look at Jesus suffering to pay the penalty of our sin. Look at the blood dripping from His feet and His hands because He was nailed to the cross. Look at the blood dripping from His head where the crown of thorns was jammed. Look at His side where He was stabbed by the javelin, and look at His whole body that was horribly beaten even before He was nailed to cross. Finally, think about the words of Jesus when He said, "Father, forgive them, for they do not know what they are doing" (Luke 23:34). I think that's a nice way of saying, "Father, they're sinful; they're stupid; they're idiots, but forgive them." The life that Jesus lived, along with what He did and what He said on the cross, and then three days later being raised from the dead strongly reveals God's love for us as John 3:16 so clearly states, "For God so loved the world, that He gave His only begotten Son, that whoever believes in Him shall not perish, but have eternal life."

God makes it clear that sin is never logical because it's illogical. For us to sin in any way makes no sense when we think about the attributes of God. Consider the following attributes of God in light of our sinful thinking and actions:

- His *love* is unconditional and self-sacrificial as Jesus demonstrated on the cross to pay the penalty for our sin.
- His *grace* is unmerited favor and God giving us what we do not deserve.
- His *mercy* is God withholding what we do deserve.
- His *patience* is God waiting and giving us time to repent and change and grow.

Think more specifically about God's primary attributes, and how illogical or stupid our sin is compared to God's character:

- His *holiness* means He is perfect, completely separate from sin, and does not have the ability to sin. Since He has commanded us in 1 Peter 1:16 "You shall be holy, for I am holy," then why do we willfully disobey God's Word?
- His *omnipotence* means He is all-powerful. God the Holy Spirit inspired Paul to write Ephesians 3:20 "Now to Him who is able to do far more abundantly beyond all that we ask or think, according to the power that works within us." Why do we doubt what God clearly states in His Word?
- His *omniscience* means He knows everything, which means He knows our thoughts, every one of them. Why do we think we can sin and nobody will know it, or we can think whatever we want but we're not accountable for our thoughts?
- His *omnipresence* means God is everywhere, so He sees everything. He communicated that truth to us in Proverbs 15:3 "The eyes of the LORD are in every place, watching the evil and good." So why do we think nobody's watching us as we sin? It's because if we think that way then we probably won't get caught sinning?

Think about what He has already done for us, what He wants to do right now for us, and what He will do for us in eternity. There's no excuse for our disobedience to God, and there's no justification for violating God's Word. Sin is stupid and unnecessary since God's Word tells us all we need to know and do for life and godliness (1 Peter 1:3). Jesus was a perfect example of how to live our lives for the glory of God by loving Him, loving others, and denying ourselves. In Luke 9:23 Jesus even said, "If anyone wishes to come after Me, he must deny himself, and take up his cross daily and follow me." To deny ourselves means to have a total disregard for our own interest. Sin is never logical! It's not logical because why would we want to think about ourselves and what we want instead of thinking about God and what He wants in our lives?

However, even though we make foolish, stupid, or illogical decisions at times, God meets us where we are spiritually, and while working "all things together for good" (Romans 8:28), He helps us to take steps of growth that glorify Him and conform us more to the image of His dear Son. But we have to remember 1 Peter 5:5 where Peter was inspired by the Holy Spirit to write, "God is opposed to the proud, but He gives grace to the humble." So we need to be humble and admit we're proud, and we need to admit our sin is never logical. It makes no sense at all to be sinful and disobedient. God will help us take every step we need to take to bring more glory to Him. He said in 2 Corinthians 12:9 "My grace is sufficient for thee, for my strength is made perfect in weakness" (KJV). If we live our lives as He instructs us from His Word, even though we sometimes make sinful, selfish, illogical, and stupid decisions, we will see *What God Can Do with an Idiot*!

CHAPTER 2

Adam: The First Human Idiot

What God Can Do with the Man by Whom Sin Entered into the World

*I*n order to solve problems, you have to discover some solutions, and part of that process involves going back to the beginning when the problems started. Of course for Christianity, all the beginning started in Genesis 1:1: "In the beginning God created the heavens and the earth." The word 'created' means to make something out of nothing. It didn't take thousands or millions of years for the earth and universe to evolve. God's Word makes it clear that He spoke everything into existence with the word of His mouth, and He did it in six literal twenty-four-hour days.

You might be asking, "What does that have to do with my life and the decisions or choices I make?" The answer is, God owns everything because He is the Creator of the heavens and the earth. Because God created man and breathed into him the breath of life, God has the authority to tell everybody what to do or not do and how to think or not think. There is a natural demand for submission and cooperation, for respect and honor, for love and obedience and commitment to the Creator from the created.

To reject the authority of the Creator, to ignore the respect and honor due to the Creator, or to refuse to love the Creator not only makes no logical sense, but it's simply stupid.

Remember, the *greatest* commandment in the Law is revealed in Matthew 22:36–38 when Jesus answered the question, "Teacher, which is the great commandment in the Law?" And He said to them, 'YOU SHALL LOVE THE LORD YOUR GOD WITH ALL YOUR HEART, AND WITH ALL YOUR SOUL, AND WITH ALL YOUR MIND.'" A good question to ask would be: What is it about that statement that we don't understand? It might help us to remember what Jesus said about this subject in John 14:15, "If you love Me, you will keep My commandments." If we don't love Him, we won't keep His commandments, and our disobedience reveals how sinful we are. Being sinful reveals how stupid we are to fail to love the One who loves us and gave Himself for us (Ephesians 5:2). Even though we were sinners and stupid, and sometimes we still sin and make stupid decisions, Jesus gave Himself for us to pay the penalty for our sin and made it possible for us to be forgiven of our sin and be clothed in righteousness as we spend eternity with Him.

In reality, Adam was the first human idiot. God's Word makes that very clear in Romans 5:12 "Therefore, just as through one man sin entered into the world, and death through sin, and so death spread to all men, because all sinned." Adam had the entire garden of fruit from which to choose and only *one* restriction to follow. God made that very clear when He stated in Genesis 2:16–17 "From any tree of the garden you may eat freely; but from the tree of the knowledge of good and evil you shall not eat, for in the day that you eat from it you will surely die." Now think about that for a moment: "any tree of the garden" was available and would meet Adam's need. However, Adam consciously, willfully, and decisively ignored those facts and plunged the entire human race into the consequences of sin which are death, an eternity in hell, and separation from God forever and ever.

Adam was an idiot for what he did, but we have to be careful and not think if that had been us, we would not have made that sinful choice! Adam proved his stupidity even more by putting on the fig leaves to cover their sin and hiding in the bushes so God wouldn't find them. Think about it ... the God who holds the universe in the palm of His hand was *not* going to be able to find Adam and Eve in the bushes? That's almost thinking like God the Father would have to ask Jesus or the Holy Spirit to help Him find Adam and Eve because He couldn't see them! I think we would agree that was very stupid on Adam's part, and that's one of the results of the curse of sin.

However, in the midst of Adam being an idiot, God still used him to fulfill His divine plan of redemption. God knew exactly what Adam would do when He breathed into Adam the breath of life and Adam became a living soul. But even knowing what Adam would do, God still created him and his wife. God used Adam as a bridge to the second Adam, and God knew there would be a day when the second Adam would be made flesh and dwell among us, and we would see His "glory as of the only begotten from the Father, full of grace and truth" (John 1:14). Jesus came from the seed of Adam, and look at what He did for us. Paul put it this way in 1 Corinthians 15:22 "For as in Adam all die, so also in Christ all will be made alive." Paul went on to write 1 Corinthians 15:26 "The last enemy that will be abolished is death." Even though death entered the world through Adam, God used Adam to make a bridge to the second Adam who would shed His blood and die on the cross to pay the penalty for our sin and in three days would conquer death and be raised from the dead to offer us eternal life.

Paul made it clear what God can do with an idiot like Adam in Romans 5:18–21 "So then as through one transgression there resulted condemnation to all men, even so through one act of righteousness there resulted justification of life to all men. For as through the one man's disobedience, the many were made sinners, even so through the obedience of the One, the many will be made righteous. The Law came in so that the transgression would increase, but where sin increased, grace abounded all the more, so that, as sin reigned in death, even so grace would reign through righteousness to eternal life through Jesus Christ our Lord." While the first Adam was an idiot, the second Adam was perfect and holy and loved us and gave Himself for us.

So even though you are not perfect either, and sometimes you are an idiot like Adam was, and you make some stupid decisions that impact your life and others around you, God can use you to spread the gospel message of the death, burial, and resurrection of Jesus Christ. Even though we are forgiven idiots, we can learn to live godly lives with God's help and glorify God in what we say and do so we can be the "salt of the earth" and "the light of the world" (Matthew 5:13–14). Even before Adam was created, God had a plan to use him. God has a plan for us even though sometimes we are idiots and make sinful choices. Focus on what God can do with an idiot like Adam, and what He can do with you, and it will give you hope to learn the lessons God wants you to learn and to press on living your life to glorify the One who loved you and gave Himself for you.

CHAPTER 3

Noah: Found Favor in the Eyes of the LORD

What God Can Do with a Man Who Got Drunk

God can use us for His glory even though He knows in advance that we are going to be idiots at times. God is omniscient—He knows everything. Matthew 9:4 states, "And Jesus knowing their thoughts said, 'Why are you thinking evil in your hearts?'" And even though Jesus knows what we are thinking in our hearts and what we are going to do today or tomorrow, He still demonstrates His unconditional love for us and shows us His amazing grace and His wonderful mercy. Even though God knows everything before the foundation of the world and for all eternity, He still uses us for His glory in spite of our sinful and selfish choices.

Genesis 6:5 clearly states, "Then the LORD saw that the wickedness of man was great on the earth, and that every intent of the thoughts of his heart was only evil continually." The results of the curse of sin, which were the result of Adam's choice, spread rapidly through the hearts of mankind. It even got to the point where Genesis 6:6 reveals, "The LORD was sorry that He had made man on the earth, and He was grieved in His heart." This doesn't mean God made a mistake. God is holy, and He does not have the ability to make a mistake. He's perfect and sinless. This verse, along with Genesis 6:7, expresses His sorrow for the sin of mankind and His love for mankind. But because of His love for the people He created, He is willing to do something about their sinful condition.

It's similar to a father disciplining his child. A father doesn't want to spank that child, and he is sorry he has to do it. But because of his love for that child, and his desire to see that child grow and change spiritually, the father will do what he knows God has instructed him to do to his child so the child will learn that choices have consequences, and he or she needs to keep growing spiritually so he or she doesn't keep making the same mistakes.

At that point in the history of mankind, God stated that something had to be done. In Genesis 6:7, the LORD said, "I will blot out man whom I have created from the face of the land, from man to animals to creeping things and to birds of the sky; for I am sorry that I have made them." However, Genesis 6:8 reveals what the LORD thought of Noah: "But Noah found favor in the eyes of the LORD." The following verses in Genesis 6 give the details for Noah to build the ark and to allow two of every living thing of all flesh (male and female of birds, animals, and every creeping thing on the ground) to be brought onto the ark, and of course, all of his family, which included his sons, his wife, and his sons' wives. Genesis 6:22 reveals Noah's character as it states, "And Noah did according to all that God commanded him, so he did." However, that's not where the story of Noah ends.

I'm sure we all could give examples of times when we obeyed God and did exactly what God had commanded us to do because we wanted to obey God and avoid the consequences of disobedience to God. Remember, Noah and his family had just seen what God did in judgment to the whole earth. After the worldwide flood, the animals were released to go out and spread across the earth, and Noah and his family got back into normal life on earth. Genesis 6:19 states, "Then Noah began farming and planted a vineyard." His choice seems normal and reasonable, considering how the whole earth was destroyed by the flood, but now things were getting back to where they used to be.

However, after that verse, something drastic happened—something stupid that should have never happened. Remember, all sin is stupid! In light of what God had just demonstrated to Noah and his whole family, Genesis 9:21 reveals an example of an idiot: "He drank of the wine and became drunk and uncovered himself inside his tent." Noah got drunk (an illogical choice after seeing God's mighty hand at work!) and took off all his clothes so he was naked. Why did he do this? What was he trying to prove? What was he thinking? God doesn't reveal specific reasons to us for this specific situation, but in light of the other passages regarding drunkenness and nakedness, Noah was an idiot. He was thinking of himself instead thinking about God who saved his life and the lives of his family. He wasn't thinking about his family and the impact this could make on them. His stupid choice, and the moment he was an idiot, made it easy for his son, Ham, to sin, which resulted in a curse being pronounced on Ham, the father of the Canaanites who have a horrible history in the Old Testament.

Evidently, Shem and Japheth knew that they were not supposed to look at their naked father, so they went in backward with a garment hanging over their shoulders and "covered the nakedness of their father, and their faces were turned away, so they did not see their father's nakedness" (Genesis 9:23). We can be sure that Shem and Japheth were thankful that they responded the way they did, instead of responding like Ham responded. After Noah woke up and pronounced the curse on Ham, he also pronounced a blessing on Shem and Japheth. This situation is another illustration of the statement, "Choices have consequences." This situation is also a reminder of Galatians 6:8 "For the one who sows to his own flesh will from the flesh reap corruption, but the one who sows to the Spirit will from the Spirit reap eternal life."

However, in spite of his upcoming choices to get drunk and take off his clothes and become naked that would create a very disastrous situation with his son, God still used Noah to build an ark that would provide protection from the flood and change the whole world and his family. In fact, the writer of Hebrews wrote this about Noah in Hebrews 11:7 "By faith, Noah, being warned by God about things not yet seen, in reverence prepared an ark for the salvation of his household, but which he condemned the world, and became an heir of the righteousness which is according to faith." Even though God knew Noah would make a decision that only an idiot would make, God still used him to bring glory to God and show the world that God can still use us in many ways even though He knows we are going to make some stupid, dumb, selfish, sinful, ungodly, idiot choices.

Has God used you in the past to bring glory to Him, even though He knew that you would make the choice of an idiot and ruin your relationship with someone or a group of people, or maybe even your spouse, or your family, or some of your friends? Remember, God knew before the foundation of the world what you would do and the choices you would make, but He still used you. You need to repent, which means to change your mind, and ask God's forgiveness, and look for ways to change and grow, and be willing to admit you were an idiot and seek forgiveness from anyone you've offended. God's not finished with you because you are still alive and reading this book. He knows what's ahead of you. And even though He knows every situation where you will act like an idiot, He can still use you to bring glory to God and make an impact on the lives of others. That could include your spouse, your family, your church, your friends, your neighbors, your co-workers, and especially those who may not even know Jesus as their Lord and Savior. So remember, God can use you, even though He knows when, where, and how (today or in the future) you will make the choice of an idiot!

CHAPTER 4

Abraham: A Friend of God

What God Can Do with a Man Who Doubts God's Promises

God's Word often refers to those who know Jesus as their Lord and Savior as children of God or sons of God. How would you like to be called, "A friend of God"? Well, guess what? In John 15:5, that's exactly what Jesus called us when He said, "No longer do I call you slaves, for the slave does not know what his master is doing, but I have called you friends, for all the things that I have heard from my Father, I have made know to you."

Every person is born a sinner, and we all came forth from the womb speaking lies (Psalm 58:3). However, if a person knows Jesus as his or her Lord and Savior, then that person's sins have been washed away by the blood of the Lamb of God. He not only calls us His children, but He also calls us *friends*. It is a great honor to be called a "friend of God" because of God's relationship to us as the Creator of the heavens and the earth. It's also a great honor because of our relationship to Him as His born-again children and as His servants. Jesus calls us *friends* because He redeemed us by shedding His blood on the cross to pay the penalty for our sin, to forgive us of our sin and wash away our sin, and to restore us to a growing relationship with God as a child of God and as a friend of God. The One who called us His *friends* also promised us a home in heaven where we will spend eternity with Him because of the redemption from our sins in the past, present, and future.

However, as we all know, human friends are not always faithful because of the effects of the curse of sin; therefore, nobody is perfect. Abraham was not perfect, and neither are we. We all face the battle Paul stated in Galatians 5:17 "For the flesh set its desire against the Spirit, and the Spirit against the flesh; for these are in opposition to one another, so that you may not do the things that you please." The only perfect and sinless person who has ever walked the face of the earth is Jesus. He never sinned. He lived a perfect, loving, and sinless life. He never betrayed anyone or did anything wrong in any way or to any person. He never said anything He wished He had not said, and He never failed to say something He should have said. He never responded to the sins or accusations from others in any way that would not bring honor and glory to His Father. He never did anything that was not consistent with the Word of God. He never turned His back on a person and refused to help a person. He never told a person to not ever bother Him again. He was a perfect Shepherd looking for ways to help sinful sheep. He lived a perfect, godly, loving, gracious, merciful, patient, kind, generous, problem-solving, forgiving, helpful, encouraging, and God-glorifying life. He is the perfect Friend! Because of the life of Jesus, God the Father could say, "This is My beloved Son in whom I am well pleased" (Matthew 3:17)

But the things that can be said of Jesus cannot always be said of us or our friends because no human being is perfect. Even though Abraham was called "the friend of God" in 2 Chronicles 20:7 and James 2:23, Abraham was not perfect. I'm sure we all could give examples of friends who said they loved us, but they also said things about us that were wrong, blatantly told a lie about us, didn't defend us when they should have, or confronted us with the truth but the confrontation was done in an ungracious manner and was lacking the obedience to "speaking the truth in love" (Ephesians 4:15). We all could give other examples of friends who didn't do what you asked them to do, even though what you asked them to do would have been pleasing to God and helpful to you in a specific situation, or in a fiery trial through which you were enduring and trying to bring glory to God in the way you responded. However, that friend chose to reject your request and do what he or she thought was right. But their choice was actually sinful because it was unbiblical, so therefore, it was not pleasing to God.

While a friend may have sinned against you, his or her sin is ultimately against God. But we have to keep this in mind and be honest; it's not just our friends who fail us sometimes, but we sometimes fail them in the same ways. Sometimes we fail our friends more often than they fail us! We also need to remember that all failures, which are stupid choices, are ultimately against God. God knows that His friends are not always right, even though they think they are right and all they do is perfect.

There are times when a friend of God will take credit for what God has done through him or her, or a friend of God will challenge others to look at the amazing results of all the excellent decisions he or she made instead of focusing on the decisions God made and the undeserved blessings He has bestowed upon all of us. Well, there's one word to describe that kind of attitude and words that truly reveal what is going on in the heart of that kind of a person: *pride*! All of our stupid thinking and our idiotic decisions are rooted in that very word, *pride*. Notice the middle letter of the word. Many times we want to do what we think is best, but we don't want to do what the Word of God commands us to do because it's the opposite of what we want to do. But after we have made our selfish decision, we face the consequences of our choice, and then we see that God was right, and we were wrong. We also come to realize that God is perfectly holy and cannot make a mistake and that we are idiots!

It's very obvious that the decisions we make reveal our true character. It's easy to make decisions when things are going our way. Sometimes we are able to avoid the things we don't want to face. When things are going well or we are able to avoid those discomforts, we tend to think God is blessing us in many ways, so we must be doing what is right. Sometimes we even think we deserve the good way God is treating us. We need to remember that God's blessings are a result of His grace, which is God's unmerited favor, so therefore we don't deserve those blessings. When we are thinking properly, we thank the Lord for all His attributes and the gracious and merciful love He has demonstrated to us in many ways.

However, the real test of our faith is when things are not going the way we want them to go, when we are not getting what we truly desire, when certain things are not happening in a timely manner as we think they should or certain things are happening in our lives that we think we don't deserve or we never thought would have ever happened in our lives. To summarize those concepts, we could use the word *impatience*, along with the biblical concept of *lacking faith* in what God has communicated and/or promised in His Word. It could also be lacking faith in what God has specifically promised to fulfill in our lives, even though He might not give us the exact time or the exact manner in which His promise will be fulfilled. Sometimes those decisions can seem to be very minor, but because we develop a pattern of impatience or a lack of faith, it can lead to other wrong decisions that are major and can have a significant impact on our lives and/or the lives of others around us. The impact could be upon our marriage, our family, our church, our ministry, our friends, our neighbors, our co-workers, or many others we already have or could possibly have a significant influence on their lives. For those who are in a governmental position, the decision could have a significant impact on our state or our country or other countries. Any one of these persons or groups of people could be seriously impacted by our wrong thinking, our impatience, our lack of godly love, our selfish choices, our desire to please man instead of pleasing God, our decisions that are contrary to the Word of God, or our lack of faith in our God who "is able to do exceedingly abundantly above all that we ask or think" (Ephesians 3:20) and our lack of trust in the "God who cannot lie" (Titus 1:2).

There's a lesson to be learned in the life of Abraham by going back to Genesis 11 when Sarai (later her name was changed to Sarah, which means *princess*) became the wife of Abram. In Genesis 12, God began to give instructions and promises to Abram (which means *exalted father*), and whose name was later changed to Abraham (which means *father of a multitude*). God instructed Abram, "Go forth from your country, and from your relatives and from your father's house, to the land which I will show you" (Genesis 12:1). The promises included God making Abram a great nation, blessing him, making his name great, and Abram being a blessing. In Genesis 12:3 God clearly stated, "I will bless those who bless you, and the one who curses you I will curse, and in you all the families of the earth will be blessed." Abram did what God commanded, even though he was not perfect in this whole process. The author of Hebrews confirmed Abraham's obedience and walk of faith in what God commanded him to do. Hebrews 11:8 says, "By faith, Abraham, when he was called, obeyed by going out to a place which he was to receive for an inheritance; and he went out, not knowing where he was going."

But in Genesis 15:4, God promised Abraham a son: "But one who will come forth from you own body, he shall be your heir." Then the LORD took him outside and told him, "Now look toward the heavens and count the stars if you are able to count them. And He said to him, 'So shall your descendants be'" (Genesis 15:5). History records that God fulfilled that promise to Abraham! But we also need to learn a very important lesson from the bad decision that Abram made with Hagar, the Egyptian maid of his wife, Sarai. In Genesis 16:2, Abram "listened to the voice of Sarai" when she told him to "Please go in to my maid; perhaps I will obtain children through her." Abraham made a bad choice—the choice of an idiot—because he had sex with Hagar.

Shortly after Hagar found out she was pregnant, she fled from Sarai's presence because Sarai was treating her harshly. While Hagar was out in the wilderness, the angel of the LORD told Hagar that she was going to give birth to a son, and she was to call his name Ishmael (which means 'God hears') because God had given serious attention to the circumstances she was facing. The angel also said to her, "I will greatly multiply your descendants so that they will be too many to count" (Genesis 16:10), and "He will be a wild donkey of a man, his hand will be against everyone, and everyone's hand will be against him, and he will live to the east of all his brothers" (Genesis 16:12).

Ishmael is the father of the Middle East who, to this day, is still in opposition to the children of Israel, the descendants of Abraham's other son to whom Sarah later gave birth and whose name is Isaac. The nation of Israel is still facing the consequences of Abraham's stupid choice resulting in the tension and strife between the descendants of Ishmael and the descendants of Isaac. Abraham should not have listened to his wife in that situation. In reality, he was an idiot regarding that decision to have sex with Hagar instead of trusting the LORD to provide him a child through his wife, Sarah. In spite of those choices, God still had a plan for His friend Abraham. God told Abraham, "Sarah your wife will bear you a son, and you shall call his name Isaac, and I will establish My covenant for his descendants after him" (Genesis 17:19).

God helped His friend to fulfill the plan that He had promised through Abraham's son, Isaac. Isaac is the father of Jacob, and Jacob is the father of twelve sons who were the twelve tribes of Israel who are God's chosen people! An example of this is in 1 Chronicles 1 where the author lists Abraham in the genealogy from Adam all the way to the throne of David and God's relationship with David, which leads to ultimately to the birth of Christ. In spite of all the decisions Abraham made, God kept His promise and used His friend to be the seed of the Redeemer who would give His life to pay the penalty for our sin and give us a home in heaven for eternity! In addition, Paul wrote in Galatians 3:6–9 "Even so Abraham BELIEVED GOD AND IT WAS RECKONED TO HIM AS RIGHTEOUSNESS. Therefore, be sure that it is those who are of faith who are sons of Abraham. The Scripture, foreseeing that God would justify the Gentiles by faith, preached the gospel beforehand to Abraham saying, "ALL THE NATIONS WILL BE BLESSED IN YOU." So then those who are of faith are blessed with Abraham the believer." In addition, Paul went on to write in Galatians 3:29 "And if you belong to Christ, then you are Abraham's descendants, heirs according to promise."

What does all this prove to us? The answer is: God also has a plan for us even though sometimes we make stupid decisions and act like idiots. Sometimes it's amazing the way God uses us after we've made some stupid decisions. But God always has a plan, and nobody can stop it or change it. God is always in control of all our circumstances of blessings or punishments. He is always in control, even in the life of an idiot making wrong decisions but who is still a "friend of God." The Lord will bless whom He has promised to bless, and He will curse those He has promised to curse, but His love will never fail!

My friend, that's what God can do with an idiot! What is God trying to do in your life to bring glory to Himself and help you to be a blessing to others around you? Remember, even though you fail and make stupid decisions sometimes, and you're an idiot, you are still a friend of God if you know Jesus as your Lord and Savior. Keep your focus on the promises of God because He will fulfill them in His way and in His time. While you are running the race, keep your focus on obeying the commands of God. Make sure your motive is to do whatever you do for His glory until He takes you home, or Jesus returns and takes us all home to be with Him forever! When either of those events happen, our idiocy is over because the curse of sin will be removed. But remember, each one of us will give an account at the judgment seat of Christ for the life we've lived. I'm sure you want to hear Jesus say to you, "Well done, good and faithful slave. You were faithful with a few things, I will put you in charge of many things; enter into the joy of your master" (Matthew 25:21).

CHAPTER 5

Moses: Drawn from the Water

What God Can Do with a Man Who Questions God's Choices and Strikes the Rock

Moses is probably one of the most popular persons in the Word of God, along with several others we are considering. What comes to your mind when you hear the name *Moses*? There are definitely things that took place in his life that have a way of influencing our thoughts about biblical history and what happened in the Old Testament to Israel, God's chosen people. We could also ask some other questions like, "What impact does the life of Moses have on the New Testament church, and what is the impact of his life on Christians today?" We can ask more specifically, "How can the Lord use the life of Moses to impact my Christian life today in such a way that I could bring glory to God even though I don't always make the right decision?" Romans 15:4 clearly states, "For whatever was written in earlier times was written for our instruction, so that through perseverance and the encouragement of the Scriptures we might have hope."

After the Israel was freed from the slavery of Egypt, they were wandering in the desert or wilderness of Zin, and there was no water for the congregation of Israel (Numbers 20:1–2). As a result, the people of Israel confronted Moses and Aaron and said to them, "If only we had perished when our bothers perished before the LORD! Why then have you brought the LORD'S assembly into this wilderness, for us and our beasts to die here? Why have you made us come up from Egypt, to bring us in to this wretched place?" (Numbers 20:3–5). They also spoke about the food this place did not have and clearly stated there was no water to drink. Moses, along with Aaron, went into the tent of meeting (known as the tabernacle, a tent where the presence of the LORD was) and fell on their faces. Then the glory of the LORD appeared to them and spoke to Moses and said to him, "Take the rod; and you and your brother Aaron assemble the congregation and speak to the rock before their eyes, that it may yield its water. You shall thus bring forth water for them out of the rock and let the congregation and the beasts drink" (Numbers 20:8). What is it about that command to "speak to the rock" that anybody could misunderstand?

Well, instead of speaking to the rock, Moses was an idiot, and he made a stupid, dumb, rebellious, and serious consequential decision when he struck that rock twice with his rod, and water came gushing out abundantly, and the people and their animals drank the water. However, as a result of that stupid decision, the LORD said to both Moses and Aaron, "Because you have not believed Me, to treat Me as holy in the sight of the sons of Israel, therefore you shall not bring the assembly into the land which I have given them" (Numbers 20:12). The LORD was referring to the Promised Land that He had promised to Abraham, Isaac, and Jacob! What an awesome opportunity Moses missed because of one stupid choice he made! Can you imagine the LORD speaking to you personally in your presence and telling you exactly what to do, and then you walk away and disobey Him and do what you want to do instead of doing what He told to do? While Moses did that, even though he heard the actual voice of the LORD, we do the same when we read the Word of God and walk away and make a sinful, selfish, disobedient, and stupid decision!

MOSES: DRAWN FROM THE WATER

We can certainly learn some lessons and gain hope from the life of Moses even though he was not perfect. He made a stupid choice, and it cost him a great price. We also can learn the lesson that one sinful choice can make a significant impact upon our lives and our relationship with God and with others around us, which can include our spouse, our children, our whole family, our church, our friends, and even our neighbors and our co-workers. We also need to admit that a lot of times we don't think about the consequences of our choices *before* we make a choice. We need to focus on Galatians 6:8: "For the one who sows to his own flesh will from the flesh reap corruption, but the one who sows to the Spirit will from the Spirit reap eternal life."

Before we are even born, the Lord knows what we are going to do, and the stupid choices we will sometimes make in spite of what He communicated to us. Shortly after Moses was born, his mother put him into a basket in an effort to save his life because Pharaoh, the king of Egypt, commanded his people that any male child born to Israel was to be put to death (Exodus 1:15–17). God showed grace to Moses by using Pharaoh's daughter to see the basket and rescue Moses from the waters, which is what the name Moses means: "saved from the water." God used the sister of Moses to ask Pharaoh's daughter if she needed some help from a Hebrew woman who could "nurse the child for you" (Exodus 2:7). God even worked it out that the mother of Moses was the person who was asked to watch over this child and nurse him!

God had a special plan for the life of Moses as he grew older by using him to get Israel out of Egypt. Moses even said to the LORD in Exodus 6:30, "I am unskilled in speech; how then will Pharaoh listen to me?" In Exodus 7:1, the LORD told Moses, "See, I make you as God to Pharaoh, and your brother Aaron shall be your prophet." Because Pharaoh would not release the children of Israel, God used Moses to communicate and demonstrate to Pharaoh the ten plagues. Those ten included the Nile River turning into blood, the LORD smiting the whole Egyptian territory with frogs, gnats (lice), flies, damage to the livestock, "boils breaking out with sores on man and beast through all the land of Egypt" (Exodus 9:9), heavy hail, locusts, darkness, and most importantly, the "death of all the first born in the land of Egypt" (Exodus 11:5). On the same day of the last plague, Exodus 12:51 confirms, "And on that same day the LORD brought the sons of Israel out of the land of Egypt."

After Israel was out of Egypt, God used Moses to cross the Red Sea on dry ground, "and the waters were like a wall to them on their right hand and on their left hand" (Exodus 14:22). Shortly after they reached the other side, God used Moses to stretch out his hand over the Red Sea, and "the waters returned and covered the chariots and the horsemen, even Pharaoh's entire army that had gone into the sea after them; not even one of them remained" (Exodus 14:28).

Even after all these special events happened, God was still not finished with Moses even though He knew Moses was not perfect and would make a decision in the future that was disobedient. Moses was a tool in the hand of God because God would also reveal the Ten Commandments to Moses and inspire him to write the first five books of God's Word: Genesis, Exodus, Leviticus, Numbers, and Deuteronomy! The LORD listened as Moses prayed for the children of Israel who made a golden calf to be their god because they didn't know what had happened to Moses because he had not come down from Mount Sinai. God used Moses to help Israel to construct a tabernacle where the Spirit of the Lord would dwell. God used Moses throughout the book of Numbers to speak to Israel and fulfill a number of specific details that God had commanded.

The author of Hebrews summarizes the life of Moses in an amazing way in Hebrews 11:23-29, which clearly states: "By faith Moses, when he was born, was hidden for three months by his parents, because they saw he was a beautiful child; and they were not afraid of the king's edict. By faith Moses when he had grown up, refused to be called the son of Pharaoh's daughter, choosing rather to endure ill-treatment with the people of God than to enjoy the passing pleasures of sin, considering the reproach of Christ greater riches than the treasures of Egypt; for he was looking to the reward. By faith he left Egypt, not fearing the wrath of the king; for he endured, as seeing Him who is unseen. By faith he kept the Passover and the sprinkling of the blood, so that he who destroyed the firstborn would not touch them. By faith they passed through the Red Sea as though they were passing through dry land; and the Egyptians, when they attempted it, were drowned."

God allowed and ordained all these wonderful things to happen in the life of Moses while knowing that instead of speaking to the rock, Moses would strike the rock, which was not a smart thing to do. In fact, the choice Moses made was stupid! But all sin is stupid, and God still used Moses to accomplish His divine plan for His people and for His glory! What does God know about you regarding your sins that you've already committed or sins that will be committing very soon? The good news is, God knows all about you, but He still has a plan for your life. He can still use you like He used Adam, Noah, Abraham, and Moses in spite of what those men did. Think about Psalm 145:8, "The LORD is gracious, and full of compassion; slow to anger, and of great mercy."

CHAPTER 6

Elijah: A Prophet of God

What God Can Do with a Man Who Fears Man More Than He Fears God

The prophet of God, Elijah, is one of the most unique men in God's Word. The name *Elijah* in the Hebrew language literally means, "My God is Jehovah." He is introduced in the Old Testament in 1 Kings 17:1: "Now Elijah the Tishbite, who was of the settlers of Gilead, said to Ahab [the king of Israel], 'As the LORD, the God of Israel lives, before whom I stand, surely there shall be neither dew nor rain these years, except by my word.'" Throughout 1 Kings 17 and 18, and 2 Kings 1, Elijah has a track record of being obedient to the word of LORD by doing whatever the LORD instructed him to do.

In 1 Kings 17:3, the LORD told Elijah to leave where he was and to go eastward and to hide himself "by the brook Cherith, which is east of the Jordon River." Elijah was obedient and did exactly what he was told to do. After the brook Cherith dried up, the LORD told him to go to a city named Zarephath and stay there because the LORD had commanded a widow there to provide for Elijah (1 Kings 17:9–10). Once again, Elijah arose and went to the place the LORD commanded him to go. It was in that place that a widow was preparing a final meal for her and her son so they could eat it and die because there was no rain in that area and everything was dying. Even in this terrible situation, God used Elijah to tell the woman not to fear because the LORD God of Israel said, "The bowl of flour shall not be exhausted, nor shall the jar of oil be empty, until the day that the LORD sends rain on the face of the earth" (1 Kings 17:14). In verse 16, that's exactly what happened "according to the word of the LORD which He spoke through Elijah." This proves Elijah was a tool in the hand of the LORD even though the LORD knew the stupid decision Elijah would make in the future.

Immediately following this, the woman's son became sick, and in 1 Kings 17:17 "his sickness was so severe that there was no breath left in him," which means the woman's son was dead! After this happened, the son's mother spoke directly to Elijah and questioned what she had to do with him as a "man of God." She also accused him of coming to her "to bring my iniquity to remembrance and to put my son to death!" But through all of this, the LORD fulfilled His plan and used Elijah to take the woman's son upstairs. Elijah laid the son on the son's own bed, and Elijah called out to the LORD, asking the LORD to "let this child's life return to him." Guess what? 1 Kings 17:22 states, "The LORD heard the voice of Elijah and the life of the child returned to him." How would you like to ask the LORD to raise someone from the dead and watch the LORD do it?

After Elijah took the boy back downstairs to his mother, the boy's mother told Elijah, "Now I know that you are a man of God and that the word of the LORD in your mouth is truth" (1 Kings 17:24). What a truthful and God-glorifying comment made to an imperfect man who was born a sinner like the rest of us! How would you like to have somebody say that about you? We all need to realize that God wants that same truth said about us. He wants each one of us to live a life that brings glory to Him as people see Him working in our lives and using us to accomplish

His will in our lives and in the lives of others. We should not only desire that statement to be said about us, but we should live a life less like an idiot and more of a life that would merit that statement being said about us. We should also give God the glory for helping us to live in such a way because without Him, we can do nothing (John 15:5), and with Him, all things are possible (Mark 10:27).

In 1 Kings 18, something very unique and amazing occurred in the life of Elijah. This situation is another example of how the LORD used Elijah to accomplish His will and be glorified by what happened in Elijah's life. The LORD commanded Elijah in 1 Kings 18:1: "Go, show yourself to Ahab." Ahab was king over Israel and married Jezebel. Back in 1 Kings 16:33, Ahab "did more to provoke the LORD God of Israel than all the kings of Israel who were before him." Ahab served Baal (a false god) and worshiped Baal instead of Jehovah, the God of Israel. Then in 1 Kings 18:17, Ahab saw Elijah and said, "Is this you, you troubler of Israel?" Elijah, while living what he stated a few verses earlier, "As the LORD of hosts lives, before whom I stand" (1 Kings 18:15), proceeded to tell Ahab, "I have not troubled Israel, but you and your father's house have, because you have forsaken the commandments of the LORD and you have followed the Baals" (1 Kings 18:18). Elijah went on to tell Ahab, "Now then send and gather to me all Israel at Mount Carmel, together with 450 prophets of Baal and 400 prophets of Asherah" (1 Kings 18:19). Elijah challenged everyone when he said, "If the LORD is God, follow Him; but if Baal, follow him" (1 Kings 18:21).

All of them went up to Mount Carmel, and Elijah challenged them to take one ox and cut it up and place it on the wood, but put no fire under it, and Elijah would do the same. Then the prophets of Baal were to call on the name of their god to bring the fire down upon the altar and consume the ox, and then Elijah would "'call on the name of the LORD, and the God who answers by fire, He is God.' And all the people said, 'That is a good idea'" (1 Kings 18:24). Well, the prophets of Baal failed as they cried out from morning to noon. The funny part is Elijah told the prophets of Baal to call out louder because their god might be busy or sleeping and needs to be woken up. But they continued even to the evening, but there was no voice, and there was no fire to consume the ox. Then Elijah built an altar with 12 stones which is the same number of tribes of the sons of Jacob, and he then filled four pitchers of water and three times poured the water on the burnt offering and on the wood! Elijah prayed, and "the fire of the LORD fell and consumed the burnt offering and the wood and the stones and the dust, and licked up the water that was in the trench" (1 Kings 18:38). As a result, Elijah told all the people to "'Seize the prophets of Baal; do not let them escape.' So they seized them; and Elijah brought them down to the brook Kishon, and slew them there" (1 Kings 18:40). Think about that: 450 prophets of Baal put to death! Imagine God allowing you to do something to prove "If the LORD is God," and we should "follow Him" (1 Kings 18:21).

Remember, the Lord knows what we are going to do or not going to do today, and He also knows what we will do or will not do tomorrow! Elijah's fear of man is revealed in 1 Kings 19. In this case, Elijah was afraid of a woman named Jezebel, the wife of King Ahab who told her "all that Elijah had done, and how he had killed all the prophets with the sword" (1 Kings 19:1). She threatened Elijah by saying, "So may the gods do to me and even more, if I do not make your life as the life of one of them by tomorrow about this time" (1 Kings 19:2). As a result, Elijah was afraid. Instead of having a fear for the great God of Israel who answered Elijah's prayer, raised a young man from the dead, and helped Elijah to defeat 450 prophets of Baal, he was afraid of Jezebel. Instead of the fear of God, this fear of man motivated Elijah to run from the problem and hide in a cave instead of dealing with the problem in a godly manner, according to the word of the Lord, as Elijah had done in the past. Proverbs 29:25 warns us, "The fear of man brings a snare, but he who trusts in the Lord will be exalted."

But keep this in mind, and let this truth be a blessing and encouragement to you and to others around you with whom you can share these truths! Sometimes even a prophet of God whom God used to bring a young man back to life and to destroy 450 prophets of the false god called Baal can still be an idiot like the rest of us and make a stupid decision that does not reveal the glory of God. That same prophet can make a decision that demonstrates the curse of sin on all mankind's ability to think and reason. It's possible for us, and for a prophet of God, to lack faith in our God even though we serve God who created the heavens and the earth and holds the universe in the palm of His hand and does miraculous things to demonstrate His omnipotence and control over all the events in our lives. Our faith and decisions should be rooted deeply in the character and attributes of God and *not* be rooted in the fear of man because all mankind is cursed by sin and does not possess the attributes of God such as omnipotence, omnipresence, omniscience, and being perfectly holy (without sin) in *all* of His attributes.

We need to always be thinking and acting in light of this question: After all the things that God had done in Elijah's life, what was Elijah thinking or not thinking in 1 Kings 19 that caused him to fear a woman and go hide in a cave? Elijah was being very similar to Adam who went and hid in the bushes—as if that was really going to solve the problem! We can't hide from God. He always knows where we are and why we are there. The amazing thing is the grace of God (giving what we don't deserve) and the mercy of God (withholding what we do deserve) that God showed Elijah by bringing him out of that cave and allowing him to continue to proclaim the truth as a prophet of God.

Then in 2 Kings 1, a fire came down from heaven and destroyed a total of 102 men. These men were there to bring Elijah back to Ahaziah (the king of Samaria) who sent messengers to go and ask Baal-zebub (the god of Ekron), if he, the king, would recover from the sickness he was facing. Elijah eventually went to talk to king Ahaziah and communicated to him in 2 Kings 1:16–17: "Thus says the LORD, 'Because you have sent messengers to inquire of Baal-zebub, the god of Ekron—is it because there is no God in Israel to inquire of His word?—therefore you shall not come down from the bed where you have gone up, but shall surely die.' So Ahaziah died according to the word of the LORD which Elijah had spoken."

Then in 2 Kings 2, a chariot of fire and horses of fire took Elijah up to heaven in a whirlwind! This event makes it possible that Elijah is one of the prophets mentioned in Revelation who will come to the earth during the last half of the tribulation, since he is one of the two men in the Scriptures who have not "tasted death" in a physical manner. In Hebrews 9:27, God's Word states, "It's appointed unto to man, once to die." Even though Elijah made a stupid decision, God still had a plan for his life, just like God has a plan for your life even though you have already made or will make a stupid decision and confirm that you too can be an idiot.

CHAPTER 7

Samson: The Strongest Man Who Ever Lived

What God Can Do with a Man Who Rejects God's Expectations

The baby boy named Samson was born in a normal way just like any other little boy, but God had something special in store for this boy, just like He has with all of us. The Bible never mentions the name of Samson's mother—only that she was the wife of Samson's father whose name was Manoah (his name communicates the idea of rest). All the details of Samson's life occurred in the context of the sons of Israel doing evil again in the sight of the LORD, so Judges 13:1 clearly states, "The LORD gave them into the hands of the Philistines for forty years." Of course, the Philistines were not friendly people to the nation of Israel because Israel was their enemy. During this forty-year time frame, an angel of the LORD appeared to Samson's mother and informed her that, even though she had never given birth to a child, she would conceive and give birth to a son. The angel told Samson's mother, "Now therefore, be careful not to drink wine, or strong drink, nor eat any unclean thing" (Judges 13:4), and when the son is born, "no razor shall come upon his head, for the boy shall be a Nazirite to God from the womb; and he shall begin to deliver Israel from the hands of the Philistines" (Judges 13:5).

When Samson was born, "the child grew up and the LORD blessed him" (Judges 13:24). As is the case with all of the examples presented in God's Word, keep thinking about this encouraging truth: God knows the stupid things we will do, and even though we are forgiven sinners who are still idiots sometimes, He has a plan for us to glorify Him in many ways!

Like most men, as Samson grew up, he spotted a woman whom he wanted to be his wife—even though she was a daughter of the uncircumcised Philistines. Samson's father and mother questioned his decision and tried to persuade him to seek a wife among the daughters of his relatives, or among the people of Israel. However, Samson's parents didn't know that this situation was of the LORD, and He was seeking an occasion against the Philistines and was going to use their son to accomplish that goal. Sometime along the way to the city where his soon-to-be wife lived, Samson's parents were not actually with him at the moment a lion attacked him. Although Samson had nothing in his hand to defend himself, Judges 14:6 states, "The Spirit of the LORD came upon him mightily, so that he tore him as one tears a young goat." Samson killed the lion because the Spirit of the LORD helped him, even though Samson's stupid decision was still on its way and Samson didn't even know it.

Shortly after the lion event occurred, Samson went to the city to talk to the woman, and he was very pleased with her. Later, while on his way back to the city to take her as his wife, he looked at a bunch of bees and honey in the body of the dead lion the LORD helped him to kill. Samson "scraped the honey into his hands, and went on, eating as he went" (Judges 14:9) and gave some to his parents, but he didn't tell them where he got it. Then Samson's dad went back with him to see the woman his son had married. While they were there, Samson made a feast which was a normal custom for the young men. At this feast, Samson made a deal with the thirty companions who were there. He was going to give them a riddle, and if they figured it out within seven days, then Samson would give them "thirty linen wraps and thirty changes of clothes" (Judges 14:12). But if they didn't give him the right answer, Samson would get the same prize. The riddle was: "Out of the eater came something to eat, and out of the strong came something sweet" (Judges 14:14).

After three days, they still couldn't figure out what the riddle meant, so they threatened Samson's wife to get the correct answer, or they would burn her and burn her father's house with fire. She cried in front of Samson and made condemning statements like, "You only hate me, and you do not love me" (Judges 14:16). In essence, she manipulated Samson, and he eventually told her the meaning of the riddle. After she was given that information, she "told the riddle to the sons of her people" (Judges 14:17). So on the seventh day, the men of the city told Samson the meaning of the riddle. Samson responded with the truth, stating that if those men had not worked things out with his wife, they would not have gotten the answer to the riddle. As a result, the Spirit of the LORD came upon Samson in a powerful way, and he went down to another Philistine city, Ashkelon, and killed thirty people and "took their spoil and gave the changes of clothes to those who told the riddle" (Judges 14:19).

However, while Samson was gone, his father-in-law gave Samson's wife to one of Samson's companions who had been Samson's friend during this time. When Samson returned to visit his wife, he found out she had been given to one of his companion. As a result, Samson responded by using three hundred foxes to carry fire torches into the fields of the Philistines resulting in a huge amount of damage. When the Philistines found out that Samson did this, they killed his wife and her father by fire. Since they had done this to his wife, Samson told them he would surely take revenge on them, but after that revenge, he would quit—and that's exactly what happened! Judges 15:8 confirms that Samson "struck them ruthlessly with a great slaughter." As a result, the Philistines sent out some people to find

Samson. Eventually, three thousand men of Judah found Samson and told him they had come to bind him so they could give him to the Philistines who were the rulers over them. At Samson's request, the men from Judah agreed not to kill him, so they bound him in ropes and took him to the Philistines. When the Philistines met him, they started shouting at Samson. Once again, "the Spirit of the LORD came upon him mightily so that the ropes that were on his arms were as flax that is burned with fire, and his bonds dropped from his hands" (Judges 15:14), so Samson was free from the ropes. He immediately found a fresh jawbone of a donkey, and Samson killed one thousand Philistine men with that jawbone. Think about it: Do you know any other man who has killed one thousand men with the jawbone of a donkey? I think I know your answer! After that happened, God supplied him with some water, and Samson's "strength returned and he revived" (Judges 15:19).

The next step in Samson's life reveals his imperfections and lack of holiness. In short, we could say Samson started going downhill. It's amazing how many times in God's Word sexual sin or immorality impacts a person's life, marriage, family, ministry, friendships, and the future of all who are involved in that sin and all those who have to face the consequences of that sin. We need to keep in mind: Immorality baits the hook of an idiot. After all the ways "the Spirit of the LORD came upon him," Judges 16:1 says, "Now Samson went to Gaza and saw a harlot there, and went in to her"—which means he participated in a sexual relationship with a prostitute. When the Gazites found out Samson was in the city, they decided to surround the place he was staying and wait for him all night so they could kill him in the morning. However, God didn't let that happen. Samson laid there till midnight, and then he got up and went to the doors of the city gate. He grabbed the doors and the two posts and pulled them up, along with the bars, and then he carried them up to the top of a mountain. Although the Gazites were trying to kill Samson, in our terms, God helped him dodge a bullet! God showed grace and allowed

Samson's life to be spared, even though Samson made a stupid decision that set him up to be killed.

The next step Samson made was the stupidest decision he had ever made. This decision revealed his idiocy in light of the LORD's expectations of him and everything that had happened when "the Spirit of the LORD came upon him." Samson loved a woman named Delilah. The Philistines told her to entice Samson and find out where his strength comes from, and how they could overpower him so they could afflict him. She tried three times to manipulate Samson, and he answered each question. But all three times, Samson proved what was done to him was *not* the real answer. As a result, Delilah accused him of deceiving her and telling lies to her. In her fourth attempt, she said to him, "How can you say, 'I love you,' when your heart is not with me? You have deceived me these three times and have not told me where your strength is" (Judges 16:15). She pressured Samson every day and seriously annoyed him. Judges 16:17 says: "So he told her all that was in his heart and said to her, 'A razor has never come on my head, for I have been a Nazirite to God from my mother's womb. If I am shaved, then my strength will leave me and I will become weak and be like any other man.'" Samson violated a rule of communication a pastor told me: *Know when to shut up!* The rule is based on the King James Version of Proverbs 29:11: "A fool uttereth all his mind, but a wise man keepeth it in till afterwards." Samson blew it and would pay the price.

At this point, Delilah believed Samson had truly revealed what was in his heart. Therefore, she contacted the lords of the Philistines to "Come up once more, for he has told me all that is in his heart" (Judges 16:18). The lords returned and brought the one thousand pieces of silver they promised to give to her. She somehow got Samson to sleep on her knees and asked a man to come and shave off the seven locks of Samson's hair. Therefore, Samson's strength left, and Delilah said: "The Philistines are upon you, Samson" (Judges 16:20). Samson woke up and said he would go out like other times and shake himself free. The problem was he didn't know the

LORD had departed from him because of the stupid decision he made in telling Delilah the secret to the strength the LORD had given him. The sad part is the Philistines grabbed Samson and gouged his eyes out because he couldn't resist since he didn't have the strength. He was taken back to Gaza and was wrapped up in bronze chains and was forced in prison to conduct a very hard type of work knows as a grinder.

However, God's promise and plan began to come back to the surface because Samson's hair started growing back. Samson was brought into a situation where three thousand Philistine people were gathered and were watching Samson. Then Samson prayed, "O Lord GOD, please remember me and please strengthen me just this time, O God, that I may at once be avenged of the Philistines for my two eyes" (Judges 16:28). Even though Samson had made a stupid decision to reveal the source of his strength, the LORD allowed him to grab two pillars on which the house was built. Judges 16:30 says, "And Samson said, 'Let me die with the Philistines!' And he bent with all his might so that the house fell on the lords and all the people who were in it."

For an idiot who made some bad decisions, God allowed it to be said of Samson, "So the dead whom he killed at his death were more than those whom he killed in his life" (Judges 16:30). At the end of his life, God still used Samson to fight the Philistines, which illustrates how God can use us to bring about change in our lives and pull down the "pillars" of rebellion or disbelief in the life of another person. We have to admit that God can still do anything He wants, even with somebody who's an idiot!

CHAPTER 8

David: A Man After God's Own Heart

What God Can Do with a Man Who Commits Adultery and Murder and Doubts His God in a Time of Crisis

David is one of the most popular and well-known persons in the Word of God. There's plenty to know about David because his name is mentioned almost nine hundred times throughout God's Word. We know a lot about David because of the specific actions the Lord allowed him to take and the way the Lord helped him to accomplish those things. There are examples of the sins of David proving that he is not perfect, but there are also many examples of God protecting and blessing him.

In 1 Samuel 13, a man by the name of Saul was currently the king of Israel. However, Saul was acting foolishly and disobeying the command of the LORD. The prophet Samuel spoke to Saul saying, "The LORD has sought out for Himself a man after His own heart, and the LORD has appointed him as ruler over His people" (1 Samuel 13:14). At that time, Samuel didn't know who would be taking Saul's place as the king of Israel. Obviously, the LORD knew David would become the king of Israel. So the LORD prepared David to fulfill that role and to glorify the LORD in

DAVID: A MAN AFTER GOD'S OWN HEART

many ways, even though He knew that David would make some stupid choices! Early in David's life, the LORD commanded Samuel to anoint David, and Samuel did it, and "the Spirit of the LORD came mightily upon David from that day forward" (1 Samuel 16:13).

Although the LORD knew David would not be a perfect king of Israel, He continued to prepare David for the position. The LORD used David in many ways to be a blessing to King Saul even though Saul continued to disobey God's commands. While being a blessing to Saul, David faced Goliath, the Philistine giant. Having experienced help from the LORD to kill a lion and a bear that attacked the sheep for which David was responsible, David spoke confidently about how the LORD would deliver him from the hand of the Philistine. As God's Word reveals, that's *exactly* what happened! David slung a rock that hit Goliath in the head, and the giant fell to the ground, and the David took the giant's sword and cut off the giant's head. Even though the LORD knew the stupid choices David would make later in his life, He still used David to accomplish this great action against one of the enemies of Israel. When David returned to Jerusalem with Goliath's head, women came out of all the cities of Israel and were singing and dancing as they played their instruments and said, "Saul has slain his thousands, and David his ten thousands" (1 Samuel 18:7). That statement displeased Saul, and he got really angry and asked this question about David, "Now what more can he have but the kingdom?" (1 Samuel 18:8). The next day, Saul slung a spear two times at David, but David was able to escape. Saul was afraid of David because the LORD was with David, but the LORD "had departed from Saul" (1 Samuel 18:12).

You might ask, "Why did all this happen?" The answer comes from 1 Samuel 18:14, "David was prospering in all his ways for the LORD was with him." The LORD proved what He could accomplish with a man like David, even though David would fail in the future in some very serious and stupid ways, which is similar to some other people God knows—hint, hint.

WHAT GOD CAN DO WITH AN IDIOT

None of us should point our finger—just look in the mirror! In addition to all these special events, David married Michal, Saul's daughter who loved David. As a result of this marriage, Saul feared David and viewed him as his enemy. However, the LORD protected David from Saul in many ways, and David had a couple of opportunities to kill Saul, but he didn't because Saul was "the LORD'S anointed" (1 Samuel 24:6).

In addition to all these situations mentioned, there are more examples of the LORD doing great things in the life of David, even though the LORD knew what "the man after His own heart" would eventually do! It's rather shocking to know what David evidentially did in 2 Samuel 11, but it reveals very clearly what God can do with an idiot. We have to be careful that we are not overly critical of David because we can be as much of an idiot, or more of an idiot, than the "man after God's own heart." Sometime after David became king of Israel, there was a time in the spring when kings go out to battle, but David didn't go. When the evening came, David got out of bed and walked around on the roof of his house, and he saw a very beautiful woman taking a bath. Instead of turning his back and walking away, which is exactly what "a man after God's own heart" should have done, David made an ungodly decision, which is also a stupid decision and makes a person an idiot! We need to wisely focus on Proverbs 22:3: "The prudent sees the evil and hides himself, but the naive go on, and are punished." We should also obey the command in 1 Corinthians 6:18: "Flee immorality." If we don't, we are not only being rebels, we are being idiots.

Since David wanted to know something about this woman, someone told him, "Is this not Bathsheba, the daughter of Eliam, the wife of Uriah the Hittite?" (2 Samuel 11:3). Being the king of Israel, David misused his authority by sending some messengers to Bathsheba and taking her and bringing her back to David's house. We all know that she *could* have said and *should* have said, "No, King David! You can punish me in whatever way you want, but I'm not going to commit adultery with you because that would be sinful and would *not* please the Lord. I would be unfaithful to my husband, whom I love very much, and he loves me. And King David, I don't want to get you in trouble with the Lord by committing adultery and being a bad example to the people of Israel and to other people who will hear about you and the life you've lived."

However, David committed an act of adultery with Bathsheba. When they finished, it was evident that she felt guilty because "she purified herself from her uncleanness," and then she went back to her home. As a result of this sinful act, Bathsheba got pregnant and informed David. As a result this information, David told Joab, one of his military officials, to send him Uriah the Hittite. When Uriah arrived, David tried to manipulate him to get some time at his own house with Bathsheba so it would look like they would have time to have sex together, and she was pregnant because of sex with her husband, not David. Well, we know Uriah didn't want to spend time at his house with his wife because he said "all the servants of my lord are camping in the open field." The next day, David ate with him and drank before him, and David helped Uriah to get drunk, but Uriah still did not go to his own house.

As a murderous act, David sent a letter by the hand of Uriah telling Joab to: "Place Uriah in the front line of the fiercest battle and withdraw from him, so that he may be struck down and die" (2 Samuel 11:15). That's exactly what happened—Uriah was killed. When Bathsheba heard about her husband's death, she mourned for him. From a human perspective, all this was wrapped up in 2 Samuel 11:27: "When the time of mourning was over, David sent and brought her to his house and she became his wife; then she bore a son. But the thing that David had done was evil in the sight of the LORD."

In 2 Samuel 12, the LORD sent Nathan to confront David and give him a list of the consequences he would face as a result of the choices he made. However, the LORD was not finished with David! Even though David's new son from Bathsheba died seven days after his birth, God blessed David with another son named Solomon. After David's death,

Solomon eventually became the king of Israel, and he wrote the book of Proverbs, Ecclesiastes, and Song of Solomon. Each book has made a tremendous impact on God's people. One of the verses Solomon wrote about being stupid was Proverbs 6:32, "The one who commits adultery with a woman is lacking sense."

We also need to remember the foolish decision David made in 2 Samuel 24 when he numbered the people of Israel instead of putting his faith in God. David admitted what he did was foolish: "So David said to the LORD, 'I have sinned greatly in what I have done. But now, O LORD, please take away the iniquity of Your servant, for I have acted very foolishly'" (2 Samuel 24:10). David even admitted he was an idiot! As a result of this foolishness, 70,000 men died because "the LORD sent a pestilence upon Israel from the morning until the appointed time" (2 Samuel 24:15). David took full responsibility for the choice he made, and he said to the LORD, "Behold, it is I who have sinned, and it is I who have done wrong" (2 Samuel 24:17). Do you understand, even in all the ways God blessed him, David still made stupid decisions and admitted he was foolish? Do you see God's plan to prove what He can do with this idiot? We need to stop and think about this for a moment: Even though David made some idiotic choices, he was used in many different ways to bring glory to God and to be a blessing to God's people.

It should be very obvious and very encouraging to know that God had a plan for David, and God also has a plan for us! It's amazing how the Lord showed what He can do with an idiot when He inspired David to write Psalm 51. Let's put ourselves in David's situation and think about what we would do if God revealed a record of our sins and told the world about our failures. We need to ask an important question: Would we communicate and live out Psalm 51 like David or make excuses to justify our choices?

In Psalm 51, God demonstrated what He can do with an idiot, and why David is known for being "a man after God's own heart." Look at the way David responded to his sin! Every person who knows Jesus as their

Lord and Savior needs to ask this question in a very personal way: Can I speak the words of Psalm 51 as if I wrote them instead of David? If the answer is yes, each one of us as an individual would personally be able to say to the Lord:

> "Be gracious to me, O God, according to Your lovingkindness; according to the greatness of Your compassion blot out my transgressions. Wash me thoroughly from my iniquity and cleanse me from my sin. For I know my transgressions, and my sin is ever before me. Against You, You only, I have sinned and done what is evil in Your sight, so that You are justified when You speak and blameless when you judge. Behold, I was brought forth in iniquity, and in sin my mother conceived me. Behold, You desire truth in the innermost being, and in the hidden part You will make me know wisdom. Purify me with hyssop, and I shall be clean; wash me and I shall be whiter than snow. Make me to hear joy and gladness, let the bones which You have broken rejoice. Hide your face from my sins and blot out all my iniquities Create in me a clean heat, O God, and renew a steadfast spirit within me. Do not cast me away from Your presence and do not take Your Holy Spirit from me. Restore to me the joy of Your salvation and sustain me a willing spirit."

Each one of us as an individual would also reveal what God can do with an idiot. Therefore, each of us would personally say:

> *"Then* I will teach transgressors Your ways, and sinners will be converted to You. Deliver me from bloodguiltiness, O God, the God of my salvation; *Then* my tongue will joyfully sing of Your righteousness. O Lord, open my lips, that my mouth may declare Your praise. For You do not

delight in sacrifice, otherwise I would give it; You are not pleased with burnt offering. The sacrifices of God are a broken spirit; a broken and a contrite heart, O God, You will not despise."

No wonder God used David to write so many of the Psalms—David repented, confessed his sin, asked God to forgive him, and he sought to grow and change. When is the last time you had a broken spirit over the sin you committed? When is the last time you had "a broken and contrite heart" before God? No matter how stupid you've been, if you will repent of your sin and confess your sin to God, He can forgive you and wash you clean by the blood of His Son, Jesus, and He can restore your relationship with Him and with other people you have sinned against.

In addition to what has already been made known, God inspired David to write several other chapters in the book of Psalms. It's encouraging to see how David's music comforted King Saul, influenced Israel as a nation, and continues to influence and to change people's lives today because the Psalms are one of the most popular books in the Bible. In Acts 4:25, David is mentioned as the author of Psalm 2, and in Hebrews 4:7, Psalm 95 is attributed to David. All of the Psalms David was inspired to write—and there were several of them—reveal the God who loved him and used him in many ways.

Even though David was an idiot sometimes, we've seen how God used David to be a blessing to King Saul, to defeat Goliath, to become and serve as the king of Israel, to be the father of Solomon, and to write several books of the Psalms. However, and most importantly, God used David to bring glory to Himself by being part of the seed for the Messiah who is the Son of God, and whose name is Jesus who loved us and "gave Himself up for us" (Ephesians 5:2). In the New Testament, Luke was inspired by the Holy Spirit to confirm that the angel Gabriel was sent from God "to a virgin engaged to a man whose name was Joseph, of the *descendants of David*; and the virgin's name was Mary" (Luke 1:27). John, who was also an idiot at a time in his life and was known as "the disciple whom Jesus loved," was inspired by the Holy Spirit to write John 7:42: "Has not the Scripture said that the Christ comes from the descendants of David, and from Bethlehem, the village where David was?" Paul (whose life revealed what God could do with probably the biggest idiot in the New Testament) was also inspired by the Holy Spirit to write, "Remember Jesus Christ, risen from the dead, *descendant of David*, according to my gospel" (2 Timothy 2:8).

Think about this: How would you like to be part of the seed through which Jesus Christ, the Son of God, would come to be born of a virgin, live a sinless life, perform miracles, die on the cross to pay the penalty of our sin and cleanse us from our sin, and rise from the dead and offer us eternal life and make us "new creatures in Christ," and reward us for the way we served Him, and provide us a home in heaven so we can dwell with Him for *eternity* and escape the fires of hell prepared for those who reject Jesus Christ as their Lord and Savior? David was a part of that process, and he is in the presence of the Lord right now! I wonder what Jesus said to him when David met Him face-to-face in heaven. I also wonder what David said to Jesus, or if he's still on his knees bowing before the Lord and thanking the Lord that the curse of sin is removed, and saying he won't do anything stupid ever again. Well, even though David would like to go back and make some different decisions, like somebody else I know and some other people I know, God still demonstrated in many ways what He can do with an idiot.

CHAPTER 9

Rahab: The Harlot

What God Can Do with a Woman Who Is a Prostitute

One of the most prominent and memorable events in the Old Testament, and in the entire history of God's people, is Israel's battle with Jericho. Joshua 1 and 2 remind us of the promises the LORD had made to His chosen people, Israel, along with His servant Moses (even though Moses didn't cross the Jordan River into the Promised Land because he chose to disobey the LORD by striking the rock instead of speaking to the rock—but we know *What God Can Do With an Idiot named Moses*). We need to focus on how God used a tool in His hand to fulfill His promise to His people, the nation of Israel, by giving them the promised property on the other side of the Jordan River—a river that the LORD parted for them, and Israel crossed over on dry ground.

Jericho was the next hurdle to deal with, and God was going to use an idiot to help Israel accomplish another step of taking over the Promised Land. Of all the people God could have allowed to be a part of the situation of Israel conquering the city of Jericho, He used a woman named Rahab who was a harlot. A harlot is a woman devoted to engaging in sexual activity with a man in order to gain payment. But even if there

RAHAB: THE HARLOT

is no payment, sexual activity with a man who is not your husband is still a sin called fornication or adultery—which is also evidence of being an idiot because both are disobedience to God and His commands, and both reveal the lust and selfishness in a person's mind and heart. Either way, a harlot was an idiot and still is because God and His Word never change.

God used this harlot to protect the two spies who came to check out the city of Jericho and went to Rahab's house and lodged there. Even though the king of Jericho was looking for these men and commanded her to "bring out the men who have come to you, who have entered your house," Rahab hid them on the roof! She gave an explanation to the king and then actually lied to king when she said, "I do not know where the men went." She knew where they were because she put them on her roof to protect them. Rahab revealed the evidence of the LORD working in her heart to help these men get safely out of the city and back to Joshua and the people of Israel to complete what the LORD had promised He would help them do.

Although Rahab was a harlot, she listened to the counsel of God and believed that the LORD was going to do what He had promised. God's Word does not reveal how she got all this information, but Rahab made the statement to the two men, "I know that the LORD has given you the land, and that the terror of you has fallen on us, and that all the inhabitants of the land have melted away before you" (Joshua 2:9). Rahab actually revealed her view of the LORD when she said to the two spies, "for the LORD your God, He is God in heaven above and on earth beneath" (Joshua 2:11). The two men and Rahab worked out a very specific agreement to protect her and her family, and deliver their lives from death when Israel returned to take over the city. After the agreement was made, she let them down the outside of the wall with a rope through her window because she lived on the wall that surrounded the city of Jericho. It's obvious that Rahab was a tool in the hand of God to help the spies who came to check out the land that the LORD had promised they would conqueror because He also promised He would help them! Even though Rahab was known for maintaining an immoral lifestyle, God used her to provide a way of escape for the two spies.

In the New Testament, the author of Hebrews was inspired to write a very encouraging statement that reveals what God can do with imperfect people who will do *what* God wants them to do and *when* He wants them to do it: "By faith Rahab the harlot did not perish along with those who were disobedient, after she had welcomed the spies in peace" (Hebrews 11:31). Also in the New Testament, James, under divine inspiration, wrote James 2:25: "In the same way, was not Rahab the harlot also justified by works when she received the messengers and sent them out by another way?" In light of all the Word of God has to say about salvation being by grace alone, through faith alone, in Christ alone, and not by works, we have to understand that "justified by works" is the evidence of her faith and the reward of her faith in what the LORD had said He was going to do with His people Israel. The LORD blessed her for what she did, which is a nice way of saying thank you for what she just did!

We have to keep in mind something that may be a reminder to you, or it may be a surprise to you. Either way, it is evidence of *What God Can Do with an Idiot* to accomplish His will. Think about Matthew 1:5–6: "Salmon was the father of Boaz by Rahab, Boaz was the father of Obed by Ruth, and Obed the father of Jesse. Jesse was the father of David the king." We know what that means: Rahab has a part in the lineage of Christ because she gave birth to Boaz, who was the father of Obed, who was the father of David through whom Jesus was born! Although God's Word doesn't state the LORD specifically rewarded Rahab by being in the lineage of Jesus because she helped the nation of Israel and the two spies, it seems very logical and obvious in the way it happened. Even though the LORD knew the kind of person Rahab was, she was still a tool in the hand of God to help Israel achieve the goal that the LORD had set for them. In a very special way and a very privileged way, she was part of the lineage of

Jesus, the One "who gave Himself for us to redeem us from every lawless deed, and to purify for Himself a people for His own possession, zealous for good deeds" (Titus 2:14).

As a result of what Rahab did in helping the spies, God brought down the walls of Jericho. As a result of God bringing down those walls, Christian songs have been written about that event. For example, "Joshua fought the battle of Jericho, Jericho, Jericho; Joshua fought the battle of Jericho and the walls came a-tumbling down." Rahab is an awesome illustration of *What God Can Do with an Idiot*. She was not perfect, but God still used her in a mighty way to help His people accomplish His will in their lives. As a result, Rahab made it into Hebrews 11 that is known for being "The Hall of Faith." Someday in heaven, we will get to talk to her and the two spies she helped.

We might not be harlots, but we aren't perfect either because we all sin in many ways. It's encouraging to know that God still wants to use us, and He still can use imperfect people like us to bring glory to His name by accomplishing His purpose in our lives and using us in the lives of others.

CHAPTER 10

Solomon: A Wise Man

What God Can Do with a Smart Man
Who Still Makes Foolish Choices

When you hear the name *Solomon*, what comes to your mind? Many people hear his name and think of the word *wisdom* or the word *smart*. Some people think of the description of his life: The most wise human being who ever lived (second only to Jesus). Any one of those answers would be a legitimate description of Solomon whom God allowed to become the king of Israel. When the father of Solomon, King David, was getting very old, he made a promise to his wife, Bathsheba, who was Solomon's mother. King David said in 1 Kings 1:34, "As the LORD lives, who has redeemed my life from all distress, surely as I vowed to you by the LORD the God of Israel, saying, 'Your son Solomon shall be king after me, and he shall sit on my throne in my place'" (1 Kings 1:29–30). The same day, Zadok the priest and Nathan the prophet were allowed to anoint Solomon as king over Israel, and then they blew the trumpet and said, "Long live King Solomon!"

In addition to what God allowed to happen in Solomon's life on that special day, think about what the LORD had in store for Solomon while knowing that a wise man can still be an idiot because no human being has lived a perfect life except Jesus. Think about this statement a man made about Solomon to King David: "As the LORD has been with my lord the king, so may He be with Solomon, and make his throne greater than the throne of my lord, King David" (1 Kings 1:37). In a lot of ways, that's *exactly* what happened in Solomon's life, but he still made some stupid decisions that revealed he was not perfect because sin affects all of us in our ability to think and reason!

As David's time of death was getting close, the LORD allowed David to challenge and encourage his son Solomon in some specific ways. David told Solomon in 1 Kings 2:2–4: "Be strong, therefore, and show yourself a man. Keep the charge of the LORD your God, to walk in His ways, to keep His statutes, His commandments, His ordinances, and His testimonies, according to what is written in the Law of Moses." Then David stated how Solomon was going to be used by the LORD to fulfill the promise the LORD made to David regarding his sons: "… that you may succeed in all that you do and wherever you turn, so that the LORD may carry out His promise which He spoke concerning me, saying, 'If your sons are careful of their way, to walk before Me in truth with all their heart and with all their soul, you shall not lack a man on the throne of Israel.'"

The LORD kept His promises through the use of Solomon, even though Solomon would make some stupid choices in his life! In many ways, we should all be challenged and encouraged by the life of Solomon because he loved the LORD and was trying to follow the teaching of his father, David. We can learn some lessons not only from the righteous choices Solomon made, but we also can learn from the sinful choices he made!

It's amazing how the LORD revealed Himself to Solomon in a dream at night and told him, "Ask what you wish Me to give you" (1 Kings 3:5). Let's be honest with ourselves and ask these questions: How would I respond if God appeared to me and asked me that question? Do I think I would respond the way Solomon did? Solomon did well and repeated all the good things the LORD had done in the life of his father, David, and then stated the good things the LORD was currently doing in his own life: "Now, O LORD my God, You have made Your servant king in place of my father David" (1 Kings 3:7). Solomon gave God credit for what was already accomplished in his life.

Then of all the things Solomon could have asked for, he made a remarkable request to the LORD in 1 Kings 3:9: "So give your servant an understanding heart to judge Your people to discern between good and evil. For who is able to judge this great people of Yours?" The LORD was very pleased that Solomon made that request when he could have asked for a lot of other things. God's response to Solomon was very positive and promising:

> "Because you have asked this thing and have not asked for yourself long life, nor have asked riches for yourself, nor have you asked for the life of your enemies, but have asked for yourself discernment to understand justice, behold, I have done according to your words. Behold, I have given you a wise and discerning heart, so that there has been no one like you before you, nor shall one like you arise after you. I have also given you what you have not asked, both riches and honor, so that there will not be any among the kings like you all your days. If you walk in My ways, keeping my statutes and commandments, as your father David walked, then I will prolong your days" (1 Kings 3:11-14).

God had an awesome plan for Solomon's life and future, even though Solomon was going to make some very stupid and selfish choices that are contrary to what God had already said to do or not to do. Solomon is another example of God's grace, God's mercy, God's love, God's patience,

God's wisdom, and God's amazing power to do something marvelous in the life of a person who is not perfect and in all honestly, is sometimes an idiot!

After realizing what God did for Solomon, it's still amazing how the LORD used him in so many ways to influence the lives of other people who came in contact with Solomon. In 1 Kings 4:29–34 God's Word clearly states: "God gave Solomon wisdom and very great discernment and breadth of mind, like the sand that is on the seashore. Solomon's wisdom surpassed the wisdom of all the sons of the east and all the wisdom of Egypt. For he was wiser than all men...and his fame was known in all the surrounding nations. He also spoke 3,000 proverbs, and his songs were 1,005...Men came from all peoples to hear the wisdom of Solomon, from all the kings of the earth who had heard of his wisdom." God not only used Solomon's life to connect with other people, but to influence other people. Talk about a "tool in the hand of God"—Solomon was one of those tools, and in many ways, a unique tool.

God also used Solomon to build the temple of worship for the LORD to dwell there. Building the temple was a special event that God did not allow David to do, but He allowed Solomon to build that special and sacred building. Solomon "overlaid the inside of the house with pure gold. And he drew chains of gold across the front of the inner sanctuary, and he overlaid it with gold. He overlaid the whole house with gold, until all the house was finished. Also the whole altar which was by the inner sanctuary he overlaid with gold" (1 Kings 6:21–22). When that project was completed, the LORD allowed Solomon for the next thirteen years to build his own house (also called a palace). The LORD also allowed Solomon to bring to the temple the ark of the covenant of the LORD which was a reminder of God's presence with His people, and His rule over them. In 1 Kings 8:20–21 God used Solomon to communicate a message to the people of Israel about how the LORD has fulfilled His promise about Solomon taking David's place as the king of Israel and building a house for the name of the

LORD, the God of Israel. Solomon also communicated that God allowed him to "set a place for the ark, in which is the covenant of the LORD, which He made with our fathers when He brought them from the land of Egypt."

After all these projects were finished, the LORD appeared to Solomon again and communicated specifically what He would do if Solomon obeyed Him: "I will establish the throne of your kingdom over Israel forever" (1 Kings 9:5). The LORD also communicated what would happen if Solomon and his sons disobeyed Him: "Then I will cut off Israel from the land which I have given them, and the house which I have consecrated for My name, I will cast out of My sight. So Israel will become a proverb and a byword among all peoples" (1 Kings 9:7). Well, now we know Solomon would make some stupid decisions and turn away from the LORD and would face the consequences of his choices.

Though the LORD knew what was about to happen in Solomon's life, He allowed the queen of Sheba to meet with Solomon and ask him some difficult questions about "the fame of Solomon concerning the name of the LORD" (1 Kings 10:1). Solomon answered all of her questions and held nothing back that he did not explain to her. "When the queen of Sheba perceived all the wisdom of Solomon" and many other positive things (1 Kings 10:4–5), then she said many complimentary statements to Solomon, such as: "It was a true report which I heard in my own land about your words and your wisdom. Nevertheless I did not believe the reports, until I came and my eyes had seen it. And behold, the half was not told me. You exceed in wisdom and prosperity the report which I heard. How blessed are your men, how blessed are these your servants who stand before you continually and *hear your wisdom*. Blessed be the LORD your God who delighted in you to set you on the throne of Israel; because the LORD loved Israel forever, therefore He made you king to do justice and righteousness" (1 Kings 10:6–9).

As a result of that meeting, the queen gave Solomon 120 talents of gold and a very great amount of spices and precious stones. Later in 1

Kings 10:23–24, God's Word states: "So King Solomon because greater than all the kings of the earth in riches and in wisdom. All the earth was seeking the presence of Solomon to hear his wisdom which God had put in his heart!" But the next step reveals truth about God and truth about the imperfections of mankind—even the smartest ones.

In 1 Kings 11, God reveals the truth that the most wise man who ever lived (whose name was Solomon) was still an idiot at one point in his life, and he faced the consequences of his choices. God still proved what He can do with an idiot, even after the idiot had been blessed in so many ways. God also proved what He can do with an idiot after that idiot has made some sinful, selfish, and stupid choices that rejected the truth of God's Word which God inspired Moses to write what God had promised: "If you obey Me, I will bless you; if you disobey Me, I will curse you" (Deuteronomy 11:27–28). God also inspired Paul to write: "For the one who sows to his own flesh will from the flesh reap corruption, but the one who sows to the Spirit will from the Spirit reap eternal life" (Galatians 6:8).

God never wants anyone to sin, but He does allow us to make our own choices. The life of Solomon is a powerful lesson for all of us because it teaches us that it does not pay to disobey. It is not enough to *start* well. We have to continually seek God's grace to *finish* well and keep running the race that God has set before us. Life without obedience to God is a dead-end street. Solomon thought that having one thousand wives and concubines would provide happiness. But whatever pleasure he gained, it was not worth the price he paid. Solomon allowed those women to turn his heart *away* from the LORD, and that was very sad because the LORD was the One who had demonstrated to Solomon so much love, grace, mercy, patience, trust, and faithfulness to a man who had asked for wisdom to live his life for the glory of the One who kept His promises and allowed him to be the King of Israel as He had promised to his father, David. And even if it was pleasurable, what Solomon did was sinful, displeasing to God, stupid, and revealed the heart of an idiot. As the wiser Solomon wrote in

Ecclesiastes 2:14, "For God will bring every act to judgment, everything which is hidden, whether it is good or evil."

We can put all these details together and come to a conclusion: God can still do some remarkable things with an idiot! Just because Solomon failed doesn't mean that God stopped using him to bring glory to Himself and to minister to the needs of others. We know Solomon was inspired by the Holy Spirit to write Psalm 72 and Psalm 127 along with three other books in the Old Testament: Proverbs, Ecclesiastes, and Song of Solomon. Regarding Proverbs, Solomon was the author of chapters 1 to 29 and composed those truths during his reign as the king of Israel for years from 970 to 930 BC. Even though Solomon had failed in different ways, the Holy Spirit inspired him to write the truth and offer wisdom, instruction, understanding, warnings, promises, discernment, judgment, and knowledge. In Proverbs 1:5–6, Solomon communicated that he recorded his words to increase the wisdom of somebody already wise, to offer advice on wise counsel and to give understanding to those who are wise so they can become wiser.

Think about how many millions or billions of people (over nearly the past three thousand years) have read those chapters God inspired Solomon to write in those Old Testament books. It's encouraging to think about how people have been encouraged, challenged, rebuked, convicted, motivated, humbled, guilty, repentant, and willing to demonstrate their love for the LORD by listening to what the LORD has to say and what the LORD tells us to do or not to do. We must obey His Word because He loves us and gave Himself for us, and we love Him and want to do what Jesus said: "If you love me, you will keep my commandments" (John 14:15). We have no idea how many people have responded to the truths revealed in those books, and as a result, God was glorified by their actions and others were impacted by those godly choices. Just remember: God used an idiot to be a blessing to others and to help them avoid making the same foolish choices. Therefore, they could be wise and do what God commands instead of being stupid and sinning!

CHAPTER 11

Jonah: The Word of the Lord Came to Him

What God Can Do with a Man Who Tries to Run from God

*I*t's interesting how often we say that we don't understand what God wants us to do. There are times in our Christians lives when we really don't understand what God wants us to do because the curse of sin has affected our ability to think and reason, or we are neglecting the Word of God because we don't want to find out what we should be doing instead of what we are actually doing. Although there are times when we truly don't understand what God wants us to do, we have to be honest and admit there are times when we do understand what God has told us to do. The problem is, we don't like what God tells us to do, so we reject His authority in our lives and do what we want to do instead of doing what we know God has commanded us to do. God calls it foolish choices and disobedience.

I hope you would say by now that if a person thinks that way or acts that way then that person is sinning and choosing to be an idiot. Nobody's life in the Bible—or in our lives today or in lives in the future—is about what he or she wants to do. Instead, life is about what God wants all of us to do, and how He can be glorified by our obedience and ashamed and righteously angry by our disobedience. It's also true that God can be robbed of the glory due Him because we reject His authority and just do what we want to do or do what we feel like doing instead of obeying the commands He has given us. Obedience to God is *always* the best and most profitable choice we can make because it glorifies Him and demonstrates our love for Him. Jesus said, "If you love me, you will keep my commandments" (John 14:15). To put it in a direct statement: Our love for God is the *root* of our lives, and our obedience to God is the *fruit* of our lives. God promised to bless us if we obey Him and to discipline us just like an earthly father disciplines his children (Hebrews 12:5–11) if we disobey Him.

The book of Jonah clearly demonstrated *What God Can Do with an Idiot*. It begins with a very clear, direct, and unquestionable command from the LORD to Jonah because the LORD wanted to use Jonah to accomplish His will in the lives of those who were living in the city of Nineveh—but Jonah didn't like it. As usual, the issue is what Jonah was going to do as a result of what the LORD told him to do. Jonah 1:1–2 says: "The word of the LORD came to Jonah… saying, 'Arise, go to Nineveh the great city and cry against it, for their wickedness has come up before Me.'" The LORD wanted to do something to the people who lived in this great city because He was observing their wickedness, and He was going to deal with that wickedness.

As many of us have heard, God has a plan, and God's plan works. God has chosen to use people like Jonah, and us, to put that plan into action and be a tool in the hand of God as He seeks to do something about the wickedness of people, or He seeks to bless people. We would expect Jonah to have responded in a wise and godly manner by getting up and doing exactly what the LORD told him to do. Instead, Jonah 1:3 reveals the idiocy of Jonah at this point in his life because "Jonah rose up to flee to Tarshish from the presence of the LORD. So he went down to Joppa, found a ship which was going to Tarshish, paid the fare and went down into it to go with them to Tarshish from the presence of the LORD."

Here's an important question: How stupid are we to think we can run away from the LORD so He can't find us and help us do what He wants us to do? The biblical answer is: very stupid! I wonder if Jonah thought about Adam trying to hide in the bushes so God wouldn't see him, or if Jonah knew what David wrote in Psalm 139:7–10: "Where can I go from Your Spirit? Or where can I flee from Your presence? If I ascend to heaven, You are there; If I make my bed in Sheol, behold, You are there. If I take the wings of the dawn, if I dwell in the remotest part of the sea, even there Your hand will lead me, and Your right hand will lay hold of me." I wonder if Jonah ever thought if God the Father, Who holds the universe in the palm of His hand, was going to find him. If not, then God the Father would have to ask God the Holy Spirit, "Where's Jonah? I can't find him!"

As God always does, He had a plan, and He puts it into action. Many times God allows us to face the consequences of the choices we make. The LORD put forth a great storm that was about to break the ship. Many questions were asked, various actions were taken, until ultimately Jonah said, "Pick me up and throw me into the sea, then the sea will become calm for you, for I know that on account of me this great storm has come upon you" (Jonah 1:12). Jonah revealed his guilt by admitting it was his fault the sea was raging. So Jonah was cast into the sea, and the raging sea *stopped*. Even at this point in Jonah's life, while he tried to flee from the presence of the LORD, God used an idiot to teach the men on that ship a lesson: "Then the men feared the LORD greatly, and they offered a sacrifice to the LORD and made vows" (Jonah 1:16). *Wow!* It's amazing that even during the time of our sinful choices, God can still use an idiot—especially one that will admit he or she is an idiot and be willing to face the current consequences of his or her stupid choices.

Jonah's choice to disobey God—and his futile attempt to run from God—resulted in Jonah ending up in the belly of the whale for three days and three nights! Imagine what that was like, if that's even possible. I think it's safe to say that Jonah didn't have a bed to sleep on or a nightlight to turn on so he could read before he went to sleep because he probably never slept. I don't think there was a bathroom with a sink, toilet, or shower. Face it—it stunk in the belly of that great fish, but it's usually in those situations that we tend to learn things that God wants to us learn. In the belly of that great fish, Jonah prayed to the LORD his God, and the final sentence Jonah made was, "Salvation is from the LORD" (Jonah 2:10). After Jonah prayed, the LORD commanded the fish to vomit Jonah up onto the dry land, and the LORD repeated His instructions: "Arise, go to Nineveh the great city and proclaim to it the proclamation which I am going to tell you" (Jonah 3:2).

How did God use an idiot in this situation? Jonah was given a second chance to be used by God to proclaim the truth that in "forty days Nineveh will be overthrown." While that's not an easy message to proclaim, it was the truth from the LORD, and Jonah proclaimed it. The result of Jonah communicating that message was "the people of Nineveh believed in God" (Jonah 3:5), and they demonstrated repentance in many ways. Even the king of Nineveh said: "Let men call on God earnestly that each may turn from his wicked way and from the violence which is in his hands. Who knows, God may turn and relent and withdraw His burning anger so that we will not perish" (Jonah 3:8–9).

The following verse brings tears to my eyes, and maybe yours, because this is an awesome example of *What God Can Do with an Idiot*. As a result of the message God proclaimed through Jonah, and the way the people of Nineveh responded, 120,000 people were shown compassion from the LORD! We can rejoice in Jonah 3:10, "When God saw their deeds, that they turned from their wicked ways, then God relented concerning the calamity which He had declared He would bring upon them. And He did not do it."

How should we respond to what happened in the life of Jonah and in the people of Nineveh? Think about this: Hallelujah... Praise God... Glory be to God on high... Amen... Holy is the LORD God Almighty who showed patience, love, grace, and mercy to 120,000 people who listened to the message from the LORD that Jonah proclaimed as the LORD told him! Maybe you can identify with Jonah because of a specific trial or testing which you are going through by yourself because your family, friends, and fellow Christians have forsaken you and don't love you anymore, or you are going through it with some people you know and love, and they know and love you. Each person should think about the correct answer to these questions:

- What has God commanded you to do that you are not willing to do?
- Are you running from the Lord or trying to hide so you don't have to obey Him?
- What are you doing right now that you know is not what God wants you to do?
- Are you doing things you want to do behind the curtain of pride, bitterness, revenge, control, or disobedience, or self-righteousness?
- Are you trying to solve a problem your way instead of solving a problem God's way?
- Why do you not love the Lord enough to do exactly what He commands you to do?
- What is motivating you to do the exact opposite of what the Word of God commands you to do?
- Are you sure that what you want is the same thing God wants?
- In light of the problem you're dealing with, what would Jesus say if He walked right up to you right now and starting talking to you?

Just because you're doing something else that God didn't want you to do doesn't mean that you won't pay a price for making the decision or the decisions you made! Jonah spent three days in the belly of a great fish, but Jonah realized what he had done and why he was in the belly of that great fish. Jonah prayed to the LORD, and the LORD showed grace and mercy to him, and look how Jonah was used to help the 120,000 people in Nineveh!

Remember, the LORD is omnipotent (all powerful) and omniscient (all knowing), and He can prepare the "belly of a whale" to teach us some lessons. The LORD can lead us to a place of repentance, like Jonah faced, and can use us to accomplish His will in our lives even though we've made some stupid choices! All of us need to remember Jonah, and don't ever try to run from the presence of the LORD because you can't hide from Him. He knows where you are and what you are thinking. Remember Jonah, and do what God tells you to do as He uses you as a tool to help others and bring glory to God. You have no idea the results that God can bring forth if you will do what He commands you to do!

CHAPTER 12

John: The Disciple Whom Jesus Loved

What God Can Do with a Man Who Wants to Call Down Fire from Heaven and Destroy People

"The disciple whom Jesus loved" is John, the son of Zebedee and brother of James. In the Gospel of John, the apostle referred to himself as "the disciple whom Jesus loved" (John 13:23). The Gospel of John is the only book in the Bible that mentions "the disciple whom Jesus loved." But that's really not an issue, because the Holy Spirit inspired the writer of the book of John (John himself) to use those words. Here are a few verses in the book of John about "the disciple whom Jesus loved":

- When Jesus then saw His mother, and the *disciple whom He loved* standing nearby, He said to His mother, "Woman, behold, your son!" (John 19:26)
- So she ran and came to Simon Peter and to the other *disciple whom Jesus loved*, and said to them, "They have taken away the Lord out of the tomb, and we do not know where they have laid Him." (John 20:2)

- Therefore that *disciple whom Jesus loved* said to Peter, "It is the Lord." So when Simon Peter heard that it was the Lord, he put his outer garment on (for he was stripped for work), and threw himself into the sea. (John 21:7)
- Peter, turning around, saw the *disciple whom Jesus loved* following them; the one who also had leaned back on His bosom at the supper and said, "Lord, who is the one who betrays You?" (John 21:20)

So it wasn't just John's opinion that he was called "the disciple whom Jesus loved," but it was a true description and a true statement because the Holy Spirit inspired him to use those words. Jesus loved the other disciples as much as He loved John, so the title simply describes what Jesus thought of John and His relationship with John. John was the "Beloved Apostle," but Jesus loved all the disciples as well, and He loves us. The title was also geared to describe John as a person and a servant of Jesus.

Even though John was known as "the disciple whom Jesus loved," he still was not perfect or sinless. John sinned like all of us do. In his situation, John revealed his idiocy with his mouth by the words he spoke. A lot of the stupid things people did are recorded in God's Word, and we could give examples of stupidity going on today! The things recorded in God's Word that were stupid are not just an action, but something stupid with a tongue. The stupidity was revealed by the words that came out of the person's mouth, which includes *what* was said, such as a false accusation, a condemning statement, self-righteous words, proud or defensive statements, lies, or judgmental words, and *how* the words were spoken.

Luke 9:51–56 reveals John's stupid question to Jesus for which John was strongly rebuked. Jesus was getting ready to ascend back to heaven, and He was determined to go to Jerusalem. But in the process, He was going to stop along the way at a Samaritan village (a group of people who historically didn't have a very good relationship with Jewish people). But the village did not accept Him into their village because they found out He was on His way to Jerusalem, and they didn't like that city or the people in it. Luke 9:54 clearly states: "When His disciples James and John saw this, they said, 'Lord, do You want us to command fire to come down from heaven and consume them?'"

As Matthew 12:34 says, "The mouth speaks out of that which fills the heart." Our mouth reveals what is in our heart. In the situation "the Beloved Apostle" was facing, he said something stupid and revealed he was an idiot. Before you say, "I would never say what John said," think about you asking God what *you* should do to somebody who made you angry, and they did not do what you wanted them to do even if what you wanted was the right thing to do and what they should have done. Consider what you've asked God to do to someone, or to a group of someones, who offended you, or treated you improperly, or threatened you, and tried to get others to reject you. What about someone who made it clear that you are to stay away from a specific person, or a specific place, or a specific event, and if you violate that request, you will be dealt with in a legal manner? Sometimes we forget Matthew 12:36, "But I tell you that every careless word that people speak, they shall give an accounting for it in the day of judgment."

The response Jesus gave James and John reveals the wrongfulness, sinfulness, and stupidity of what John said. In Luke 9:55–56, Jesus turned around and literally rebuked them and said, "You do not know what kind of spirit you are of, for the Son of Man did not come to destroy men's lives, but to save them." It's like Jesus saying to them, "Guys, you're missing the point: I came to save the lives of people, not to destroy them—you idiots, so don't be asking to call down fire to destroy these people!"

Stupidity can be revealed by *what* we say because Luke 6:45 clearly states: "The good man out of the good treasure of his heart brings forth what is good; and the evil man out of the evil treasure brings forth what is evil; for his mouth speaks from that which fills his heart." That was the case for John, "the disciple whom Jesus loved." We also need to keep in mind that stupidity can also be revealed by *how* a person speaks. A wise person will speak the truth with love or grace or mercy or kindness or gentleness or patience or humility. Instead, a stupid person's speech will be done in pride, bitterness, revenge, hatred, disrespect, unlovingness, unkindness, impatience, condemnation, defensiveness, sinful anger, and spoken with a loud voice to threaten the listener with ungodly words and manipulation!

However, John is another example of *What God Can Do with an Idiot*. Jesus rebuked John, and later—even though John also "forsook Him and fled" like all the other disciples—God the Holy Spirit inspired John to write five books in the New Testament, which includes some of the most well-known verses in the Bible. For example, the Gospel of John has one of the most popular verses in the whole Bible, John 3:16: "For God so loved the world, that He gave His only begotten Son, that whoever believes in Him shall not perish, but have eternal life." In addition to John 3:16, think about these very well-know verses the Holy Spirit inspired John to write even though John wanted to ask that *"fire be called down from heaven…"* God can use an idiot to write the verses:

- If we confess our sins, He is faithful and righteous to forgive us our sins and to cleanse us from all unrighteousness. (1 John 1:9)
- Do not love the world nor the things in the world. If anyone loves the world, the love of the Father is not in him. For all that is in the world, the lust of the flesh and the lust of the eyes and the boastful pride of life, is not from the Father, but is from the world. The world is passing away, and also its lusts; but the one who does the will of God lives forever. (1 John 2:15–17)
- We know that we have passed out of death into life, because we love the brethren. He who does not love abides in death. Everyone who hates his brother is a murderer; and you know that no murderer has eternal life abiding in him. We know love by this, that He laid down His life for us; and we ought to lay down

our lives for the brethren. But whoever has the world's goods, and sees his brother in need and closes his heart against him, how does the love of God abide in him? Little children, let us not love with word or with tongue, but in deed and truth. (1 John 3:14–18)

- There is no fear in love; but perfect love casts out fear, because fear involves punishment, and the one who fears is not perfected in love. (1 John 4:18)
- These things I have written to you who believe in the name of the Son of God, so that you may know that you have eternal life. (1 John 5:13)
- I have no greater joy than this, to hear of my children walking in the truth. (3 John 4)
- And if anyone's name was not found written in the book of life, he was thrown into the lake of fire. (Revelation 20:15)
- And He will wipe away every tear from their eyes; and there will no longer be any death; there will no longer be any mourning, or crying, or pain; the first things have passed away. Revelation 21:4)

While the inspiration of God's Word is complete, and He inspired John to write five of the books, God wants us to not only live an obedient life according to His Word, but He also wants us to proclaim His Word. He wants us to live and proclaim the gospel to those who don't know Jesus as their Lord and Savior. Look for a way you can share John 3:16 with someone today. Look at that person and imagine them being in Hell forever where "the worm does not die and the fire is not quenched" (Mark 9:44). God might allow you to lead that person to a saving knowledge of Jesus Christ! God also wants us to obey His Word and to share His Word with our brothers and sisters in Christ to encourage them, to admonish them, to rebuke them if they are sinning, to build them up, to help them take steps of growth in thinking and acting like Christ, and to give biblical advice to people so they don't make a stupid choice and live contrary to the Word of God by doing something God commands us not to do, or not doing something God commands us to do. Think about how God used John, the disciple whom Jesus loved, and rejoice in *What God Can Do with an Idiot* because God wants to use you for His glory.

CHAPTER 13

Peter: The Rock

What God Can Do with a Man Who Curses, Swears, and Denies Christ Three Times

Peter is one of the most interesting persons in God's Word. He is mentioned many times in the New Testament and was involved in numerous activities with Jesus and the other disciples. It all started when Jesus was walking along the Sea of Galilee, and He saw Peter (along with his brother Andrew) casting a net into the water because Peter was a fisherman. Jesus made a very defining statement that captured Peter's attention. Jesus said, "Follow Me, and I will make you fishers of men" (Mark 1:17). Peter didn't ask any questions, tell Jesus that he needed to think about it for a couple of days and pray about it, or seek someone else's advice and then get back to Him. Peter immediately understood what Jesus meant, and Peter's actions demonstrated that impacting the lives of people is far more important than catching a bunch of fish. In that situation, he was smart! Peter and his brother immediately dropped their nets and followed Jesus and became members of the twelve disciples with whom Jesus spent three years in public ministry before He ascended back to heaven. We know from God's Word that even though Peter would make some stupid decisions along the way, God would use him to make a godly impact on the lives of many people. God's Word reveals that He wants to do the same things with us.

It's amazing the things that Peter observed in the life and ministry with Christ and the situations in which he was allowed to participate or respond. For example, since the creation of Adam, and even until now, how many people have been able to walk on water? The answer is: two people. Jesus was the first person, and Peter was the second. As Jesus was walking on the stormy water with the wind and waves, He approached Peter and the other disciples in the boat, and Peter said, "Lord, if it is You, command me to come to You on the water" (Matthew 14:28). Jesus told him to come, and Peter got out of the boat and started walking on the water toward Jesus. Imagine that for a few seconds—walking on top of the water like it was a road. However, like the rest of us would have probably done, instead of keeping his eyes on Jesus, Peter started looking at the wind and waves and started to sink because he took his eyes off Jesus! He cried out to Jesus, "Lord, save me!" Of course, Jesus stretched out His hand and pulled him up out of the water and then asked Peter a question: "You of little faith, why did you doubt?" As it did with Peter, and as it does with all of us, doubting Jesus is a stupid choice and reveals the lack of faith in Him who can walk on water and instantly calm the raging sea with the words of His mouth and give sight to the blind, renewing the hearing of the deaf and making the lame to walk and raising a person from the dead! In spite of Peter's lack of faith and doubting, God still had a plan for the only other person who has ever walked on water!

At another point in Peter's life, he was with Jesus and all the disciples when Jesus asked, "Who do people say the Son of Man is?" All the disciples responded with multiple answers, but Jesus got more specific and asked them, "But who do you say that I am?" It was Peter who answered with a true and powerful statement: "You are the Christ, the Son of the Living God" (Matthew 16:16). Even though Jesus knew Peter was going to make some stupid decisions in the near future, Jesus still made an awesome statement about what He was going to do with the life of an idiot who would deny Him three times. Jesus said to Peter, "I also say to you that you are Peter, and upon this rock I will build My church; and the gates of Hades will not overpower it" (Matthew 16:18). I believe "this rock" is the statement Peter made to Jesus: "You are the Christ, the Son of the Living God." Jesus went on to say to Peter: "I will give you the keys of the kingdom of heaven; and whatever you bind on earth shall have been bound in heaven, and whatever you loose on earth shall have been loosed in heaven" (Matthew 16:19).

What an awesome example of *What God Can Do with an Idiot* who was about to make some other stupid decisions. But it doesn't stop there! Jesus told all the disciples that He was going to Jerusalem to suffer many things and be crucified, and then He would be raised from the dead in three days. We refer to that as "The Gospel"—the death, burial, and resurrection of Christ. After Jesus told them about what was going to happen, it's amazing that Peter took Jesus aside and rebuked Him!

If we could go back and be in that situation, knowing what we know now, we would say to Peter, "Wait a minute, Peter. You're talking to Jesus, the Son of God, the third person of the Trinity, and the Savior and Redeemer of the world. He said, 'I am the Way, the Truth, and the Life, and no one comes to the Father but through Me' (John 14:6). You need to be careful what you say to Him and how you say it, and don't say something stupid! How can you tell Jesus that He's wrong, and what He said would happen is not going to happen?"

But in Matthew 16:22, Peter made a stupid decision when he took Jesus away separately and started rebuking Him by saying, "God forbid it, Lord! This shall never happen to You." The response given by Jesus reveals the idiocy of Peter: "Get behind Me, Satan! You are a stumbling block to Me; for you are not setting your mind on God's interests, but man's" (Matthew 16:23).

WHAT GOD CAN DO WITH AN IDIOT

God's interest is the plan of redemption through the death, burial, and resurrection of His only begotten Son, Jesus Christ. Through that plan, God is demonstrating His love for us through Christ, even though we are sinners. God's interest is based on His love for us, so we ought to be loving other people even when they sin, or wrong us, or don't love us, or they hate us and want to kill us. God's love never fails, and neither should our love fail—and it won't, if we have the mind of Christ and focus on God's interests instead of man's interest like Peter was doing. Man's interest is pride, which results in self-protection, exalting ourselves instead of God, boasting about what we've accomplished or the results we have produced, and wanting what we want instead of what God wants. We talk about showing love to individuals, but we don't do it, and we still expect people to love us as much or more than we love them. However, Jesus still had a plan for Peter, and He continued to build His relationship with a man who was going to do some other stupid things, one of them being the stupidest thing Peter could have ever done.

There were many other situations in Peter's life where Jesus demonstrated love and patience for Peter, even though Peter was not perfect and made some stupid choices. Those situations should remind us that God has a plan for each one of us, and even though we make some stupid decisions like Peter made, God still loves us and still has a plan for us. One of those personal experiences Peter had with Jesus occurred when Jesus took Peter, James, and John up on a high mountain where they experienced the transfiguration of Jesus (Matthew 17). The face of Jesus shone like the sun, and the clothes He was wearing became white as light, and Moses and Elijah were there talking to Jesus. Then Peter started talking to Jesus about building some tabernacles on the mountain for Him, Moses, and Elijah. There was a bright cloud that was overshadowing them, and a voice out of the cloud said, "This is My beloved Son, with whom I am well-pleased; *listen to Him*!" As the Word

PETER: THE ROCK

of God reveals to us, Peter was an idiot on some occasions and did not listen to Jesus, especially in one particular situation.

One of the most interesting details in God's Word is the example of how many times God, or in this case Jesus Himself, would tell somebody what was going to happen or not happen, and that person would disagree. To disagree with God is really stupid because we are telling a holy God (who is perfect and cannot make a mistake, and who is omniscient, which means He knows everything) that He is wrong, and we are right! As soon as what we call the Last Supper ended, a clear example of that happened when Jesus took all the disciples to the Mount of Olives. He told the disciples "You will all fall away because of Me this night, for it is written, 'I will strike down the shepherd, and the sheep of the flock shall be scattered'" (Matthew 26:31).

Think carefully about what Peter said to Jesus and how Jesus responded. Peter said, "Even though all may fall away because of You, *I will never fall away*" (Matthew 26:33). Jesus informed Peter, "Truly I say to you that this very night, before a rooster crows, *you will deny Me three times*" (Matthew 26:34). It's amazing that Peter disagreed with Jesus again! Even though Peter was recently told on the Mount of Transfiguration to "listen to Him," Peter still said to Jesus, "Even if I have to die with you, I will not deny you" (Matthew 26:35). I hope that reminds all of us of Proverbs 16:18: "Pride goes before destruction, and a haughty spirit before stumbling." It interesting that all the other disciples said the same thing Peter said, but it's even more interesting that later it was said of all the disciples, "They all forsook Him and fled" (Matthew 26:56). We have to be honest and admit that Peter wasn't the only idiot. All the disciples were all idiots in this situation, especially Judas, who betrayed Jesus for thirty pieces of silver and then went and committed suicide by hanging himself.

As Peter's life continued with his relationship and responses to Jesus, Peter demonstrated some further stupid choices, along with his fellow disciples. Peter and all the other disciples were taken by Jesus to the garden of Gethsemane to pray. When they arrived, Jesus took Peter, James, and John a little farther into Gethsemane and asked them to stay there and keep watch with Him while He went a little farther into the garden to pray to His Father. Jesus came back three times to Peter, James, and John, and all three times all of them were asleep! The first time Jesus came back and found them sleeping, He said to Peter, "So, you men could not keep watch with Me for one hour? Keep watching and praying that you may not enter into temptation; the spirit is willing, but the flesh is weak" (Matthew 26:41–42). Jesus went back and prayed and came back a second time and found them sleeping instead of doing what He had asked them to do. Then Jesus came the third time, and He found them doing the same thing, and He said to them, "Behold, the hour is at hand and the Son of Man is being betrayed into the hands of sinners. Get up, let us be going; behold, the one who betrays Me is at hand" (Matthew 26:45–46).

At that point Judas (one of many idiots God used to fulfill the plan of redemption) approached Jesus, along with a large crowd carrying swords and clubs. Since Judas made the commitment that the one he would kiss was the one to seize, he immediately approached Jesus. I can't even think of words to describe what Jesus said to the idiot named Judas who was betraying Christ for thirty pieces of silver. As God's Word records, Jesus said, *"Friend*, do what you have come for" (Matthew 26:50). Think of all the things Jesus could have said to Judas. Or maybe think about some of the things you and I would have said if we were in the shoes of Jesus … never mind, don't even think about it; it would probably be stupid! As they came and laid hands on Jesus to take Him to be crucified, Peter pulled out his sword and cut off the ear of Malcus, the slave of the high priest. When you think about what Jesus told Peter, it was another idiotic choice Peter made. Jesus told him to put his sword away because "those who take up the sword shall perish by the sword" (Matthew 26:52), and then Jesus asked him a few questions:

- "The cup which the Father has given Me, shall I not drink it?" (John 18:11). "Or do you think that I cannot appeal to My Father, and He will at once put at My disposal more than twelve legions of angels? How then will the Scriptures be fulfilled, which say that it must happen this way" Matthew 26:53-54

Since a legion is equal to six thousand troops, Jesus's Father could have provided *more* than seventy-two thousand angels. As we all do, we prove we are idiots because we don't think right. Specifically, we don't have the mind of Christ, because if we did, we would *act* like Christ. But our Lord and Savior Jesus Christ picked up the ear of Malcus that Peter had cut off, and Jesus put it back where it belonged—in other words, Jesus healed it! I wonder what Malcus thought about that action. God doesn't reveal how Malcus responded to what Jesus did, but maybe God used that to remind him of Jesus's love and grace for him. It wouldn't surprise me if someday we meet Malcus in heaven. That's another way that proves *What God Can Do with an Idiot*—God can demonstrate His love, grace, mercy, kindness, thoughtfulness, tender heart, and power even though we've done something stupid or are about to do something stupid.

At this point, the soldiers and the mob took Jesus away so He could be judged and crucified on the cross. The rest of the story is very well known, and we can all identify to some degree with the idiocy of *all* the disciples who forsook Him and ran away from the situation—including Peter. However, even though Peter forsook Jesus and fled, he continued to follow Jesus at a distance to the courtyard of the high priest. I think he was feeling a bit guilty about what Jesus had already told him, but he still denied it in his heart. While Jesus was going through all the suffering on the inside, Peter kept his distance from Jesus, and he even sat down with the officers in the middle of the courtyard to see what was going to happen to Jesus. As Luke 22 records the details, Peter was confronted three times about being a man who was with Jesus. But as we know, Peter rebuffed that accusation with his first denial by saying,

"Woman, I do not know Him." Shortly after that happened, a man said, "You are one of them too," but Peter responded with his second denial: "Man, I am not!" Then finally, about an hour later, another man began to state very strongly, "Certainly this man also was with Him, for he is a Galilean too." Peter responded with his third denial: "Man, I don't know what you are talking about." Immediately, as Peter was speaking his third denial, the rooster crowed!

Please think carefully about what happened next: "The Lord turned and looked at Peter" (Luke 22:61). Please, stop and think about that for a few minutes. Jesus told Peter exactly what would happen, but Peter denied it. And now that it happened as Jesus said it would, the rooster crowed and Jesus looked at Peter! I'll be honest with you, just about every time I think about Jesus looking at Peter when the rooster crowed, I start crying and thinking about what would I do if Jesus looked at me like that—especially after I denied Him three times. We know that Peter "went out and wept bitterly" (Luke 22:62). Peter "wept bitterly" because he was guilty and brokenhearted over the fact that he was wrong! But wait a minute, think about what Jesus said in Luke 22:31–32: "Simon, Simon, behold, Satan has demanded permission to sift you like wheat; but I have prayed for you, that *your faith may not fail*; and you, *when once you have turned again*, strengthen your brothers."

Satan not only wants to make us idiots; he wants to destroy our lives! Satan wants us to have no chance to turn back and strengthen our brothers, whom Satan is trying to destroy just like he is trying to destroy our lives. Satan does not want us to be in a position to share the gospel with other people whom God brings across our path—people who will go to hell if they don't repent and confess Jesus as their Savior and Lord and believe that Jesus died, was buried, and rose again. Satan wants to destroy our lives and our testimony for our Lord and Savior, Jesus Christ. But in spite of what Satan wanted, Peter repented by doing what Jesus said: "when you have turned back…" While Peter was an idiot in some situations, he finally admitted it, and he trusted the Lord to forgive him and use him to bring glory to One who shed His blood to pay the penalty for his sins (and all of our sins) and who was raised from the dead to offer eternal life to all those who believe.

Here's the point I believe God wants all of us to understand and learn from: in spite of all the stupid things Peter did, he admitted he was wrong, and he turned back and learned some lessons. As a result, guess what God did with this idiot named Peter? After Jesus rose from the dead and ascended back to heaven, God used Peter to preach a message on the day of Pentecost. If you want to do more study on all the details of this special event, read Acts 2. This was a special time where everyone present "came together, and were bewildered because each one of them was hearing them speak in his own language" (Acts 2:6). So when Peter preached, God allowed everyone there to hear in their own language and understand the message Peter delivered. As a result of the message Peter preached, "those who had received his word were baptized; and that day there were added about three thousand souls" (Acts 2:41). That's right: three thousand people came to know Jesus Christ as their Lord and Savior in the process of God demonstrating what He can do with an idiot! Their sins were forgiven because of their faith in the truth of the message Peter preached, which included the gospel: the death, burial, and resurrection of Jesus Christ.

Think about this incredible demonstration of God's grace and mercy to those three thousand people, and to Peter who had recently denied Christ three times especially in light of some of the other stupid choices Peter had made. As you read the following verses from Acts 2, think about how God used Peter to help these three thousand people take spiritual steps of growth. Think about what God can do with us if we will respond to our sin like Peter did:

> They were continually devoting themselves to the apostles' teaching and to fellowship, to the breaking of bread and to prayer. Everyone kept feeling a sense of awe; and many

wonders and signs were taking place through the apostles. And all those who had believed were together and had all things in common; and they began selling their property and possessions and were sharing them with all, as anyone might have need. Day by day continuing with one mind in the temple, and breaking bread from house to house, they were taking their meals together with gladness and sincerity of heart, praising God and having favor with all the people. (Acts 2:42-46).

And here's the final comment made regarding the day of Pentecost: "And the Lord was adding to their number day by day those who were being saved" (Acts 2:47). We have no idea how many other people came to know Christ as a result of three thousand people spreading and living the gospel. Think about how God used an idiot named Peter to make this happen. God could have used someone else, but He chose to use Peter! How does God want to use you to help others come to know Christ as their Savior?

In addition to the day of Pentecost, Acts 3 also reveals another example of *What God Can Do with an Idiot*. Peter and John were walking together on their way to the temple, and they came across a lame beggar who had been in this condition since he was born. In fact, he was being carried, and it was said "they used to set him down every day at the gate of the temple which is called Beautiful, in order to beg alms of those who were entering the temple" (Acts 3:2). An "alm" is a gift of charity, so he asked Peter and John to give him some alms. Peter's response was awesome, and God demonstrated again what He can do with an idiot. Peter told the man he did not have anything to give him, but in Acts 3:6, Peter said, "What I do have, I give to you: In the name of Jesus Christ the Nazarene—walk!" Acts 3:7-8 tells us exactly what Peter did: "And seizing him by the right hand, he raised him up; and immediately his feet and his ankles were strengthened. With a leap, he stood upright and began to walk; and he

PETER: THE ROCK

entered the temple with them, walking and leaping and praising God." Word got out that the man was healed, and all the people were watching him as he walked. They heard him praising God, and "they were filled with wonder and amazement at what had happened to him" (Acts 3:10).

At that point, Peter starting preaching another sermon about God's power and the power of the name of Jesus who God raised from the dead. He preached how that power was used to heal the lame man they were watching and how the people who were listening to Peter were the ones who crucified Jesus. Peter clearly preached a message for them to repent so their sins could be forgiven. As a result, Peter and John got thrown into jail. However, the good news is that many of them who heard Peter's sermon believed the message of the gospel. No matter how you interpret the "5,000 men" (as two thousand more converts along with the three thousand from the day of Pentecost for a grand total of five thousand; or the five thousand men as totally new converts for a grand total of eight thousand new believers from Pentecost and the lame man's healing), the point is that more people came to know Jesus as their Savior. And in Acts 4:12, Peter stated one of the best-known verses in God's Word, "And there is salvation in no one else; for there is no other name under heaven that has been given among men by which we must be saved." This strongly demonstrates *another* example of *What God Can Do with an Idiot* named Peter.

But having presented all this about Peter, there is one more example we need to focus on and be encouraged by what God did with him. Even though Peter made some stupid decisions, God the Holy Spirit also inspired (which literally means "God-breathed") Peter to write two books in the New Testament. One of those key verses the Holy Spirit inspired Peter to write was 2 Peter 1:21: "For no prophecy was ever made by an act of human will, but men moved by the Holy Spirit spoke from God." Peter was "moved by the Holy Spirit" to write a phrase in 1 Peter 5:10 that is not used anywhere else in the Word of God. The phrase is a description of

WHAT GOD CAN DO WITH AN IDIOT

God: "the God of all grace." The word "grace" is God's unmerited favor, and Peter understood the meaning of grace and how God showed grace to him in many ways! God also used Peter to write some very familiar verses in God's Word:

> In this you greatly rejoice, even though now for a little while, if necessary, you have been distressed by various trials, so that the proof of your faith, being more precious than gold which is perishable, even though tested by fire, may be found to result in praise and glory and honor at the revelation of Jesus Christ. (1 Peter 1:6–7)

> As obedient children, do not be conformed to the former lusts which were yours in your ignorance, but like the Holy One who called you, be holy yourselves also in all your behavior; because it is written, "You shall be holy, for I am holy." (1 Peter 1:14–16)

> But you are a chosen race, a royal priesthood, a holy nations, a people from God's own possession, so that you may proclaim the excellencies of Him who has called you out of darkness into His marvelous light. (1 Peter 2:9)

> For you have been called for this purpose, since Christ also suffered for you, leaving you an example for you to follow in His steps. (1 Peter 2:21)

> In the same way, you wives be submissive to your husbands so that even if any of them are disobedient to the word, they may be won without a word by the behavior of their wives. (1 Peter 3:1)

> You husbands in the same way, live with your wives in an understanding way, as with someone weaker, since she is a

woman, and show her honor as a fellow heir of the grace of life, so that your prayers will not be hindered. (1 Peter 3:7)

Above all, keep fervent in your love for one another, because love covers a multitude of sins. (1 Peter 4:8)

Therefore, humble yourselves under the mighty hand of God, that He may exalt you at the proper time. Casting all your cares upon Him, because He cares for you. (1 Peter 5:6–7)

Be of sober spirit, be on the alert. Your adversary, the devil, prowls around like a roaring lion, seeking someone to devour. But resist him, firm in your faith, knowing that the same experiences of suffering are being accomplished by your brethren who are in the world. After you have suffered for a little while, the God of all grace, who called you to His eternal glory in Christ, will Himself perfect, confirm, strengthen and establish you. (1 Peter 5:8–10)

But the day of the Lord will come like a thief in which the heavens will pass away with a roar and, and the elements will be destroyed with intense heat, and the earth and its works will be burned up. (2 Peter 3:10)

But grow in grace and knowledge of our Lord and Savior Jesus Christ. To Him be the glory, both now and to the day of eternity. (2 Peter 3:18)

Wow! Think about what God did with an idiot named Peter, and how that proves *What God Can Do with an Idiot*. Someday we'll meet Peter and give him a hug and say, "Thanks for not quitting even though sometimes you were an idiot like *me*, but I was a *worse* idiot than you!"

CHAPTER 14

Paul: From Saul to Paul

What God Can Do with a Man Who Shed Innocent Blood

Before Paul knew Christ and before his named was changed from Saul to Paul, he watched Stephen, "a man full of faith and the Holy Spirit" (Acts 6:5), get stoned to death. Prior to the stoning, it is recorded that the apostles prayed for Stephen, and they laid their hands on him (and some other men). As a result of this special blessing from the Lord through the hands of the apostles:

> The Word of God kept on spreading and the number of the disciples continued to increase greatly in Jerusalem, and a great many of the priests were becoming obedient to the faith, and Stephen, full of grace and power, was performing great wonders and signs among the people. (Acts 6:7–8)

As soon as Stephen finished the message he was preaching, a group of men who were opposed to Stephen and the truth he preached, were all "cut to the quick, and they began gnashing their teeth" at Stephen (Acts 7:54). As a reaction to the truth they heard, "they cried out with a loud voice, and covered their ears, and rushed at him" and drove Stephen "out of the city and began to stone him; and the witnesses laid aside their robes at the feet of a young man named Saul" (Acts 7:57–58). While Stephen was being stoned to death, it is recorded in Acts 7:59–60, "He called on the Lord and said, 'Lord Jesus, receive my spirit!' Then falling on his knees, he cried out with a loud voice, 'Lord, do not hold this sin against them!' Having said this, he fell asleep," which means he died and was taken to heaven to be with the Lord! Later on, and ironically, Paul would write under the inspiration of the Holy Spirit, "We are confident, I say, and willing rather to be absent from the body, and to be present with the Lord" (2 Corinthians 5:8). Sadly and stupidly, Saul totally ignored the godly responses Stephen demonstrated. A good lesson for all of us is be careful how we respond to godly people because God is using them to help us take the next step in our spiritual lives. How we respond reveals the genuineness of our hearts or the stupidity of our thinking.

One of the major idiotic parts of Saul's life is revealed by his attitude toward Stephen's death when "Saul was in hearty agreement with putting him to death" (Acts 8:1). It's very interesting that on same day Stephen was stoned to death "a great persecution began against the church in Jerusalem, and they were all scattered throughout the regions of Judea and Samaria, except the apostles" (Acts 8:2). The next verse reveals the sinfulness and the idiocy of the man named Saul. Acts 8:3 clearly states, "But Saul began ravaging the church, entering house after house, and dragging off men and women, he would put them in prison." Saul (soon to be Paul) didn't know yet that when you mess with God's people, you are actually messing with God, who is all-powerful and can destroy anything, or anybody, with the word of His mouth! But God is also a gracious, merciful, and loving God who had already sent His Son, Jesus, to die on the cross and pay the penalty for our sin and offer us eternal life!

We don't know how long it was between the details of stoning Stephen and the beginning of persecuting the church to the time recorded in Acts 9 when Saul was "still breathing threats and murder against the disciples of the Lord." He got permission from the high priest to continue persecuting the church by binding up people and bringing them to Jerusalem, which means they would be put into prison and treated harshly. But to prove *What God Can Do with an Idiot*, we see in Acts 9 how God brought about Saul's salvation as Saul was traveling on the road to the city of Damascus to further persecute God's people. After flashing a light from heaven around him and telling Saul, "I am Jesus whom you are persecuting," and taking away Saul's eyesight, the Lord used a man by the name of Ananias to communicate what Saul must do to make things right.

However, Ananias questioned the Lord about being asked to do these things. It's amazing what the Lord told Ananias about Saul: "Go, for he is a chosen instrument of Mine, to bear My name before the Gentiles and kings and the sons of Israel; for I will show him how much he must suffer for My name's sake" (Acts 9:15–16). Ananias obeyed the Lord and told Saul, "Brother Saul, the Lord Jesus, who appeared to you on the road by which you were coming, has sent me so that you may regain your sight and be filled with the Holy Spirit" (Acts 9:17). Saul's eyesight was restored immediately, and Saul was baptized and spent the next several days with the disciples who were in Damascus. The following verse is another example of *What God Can Do with an Idiot* because Acts 9:20 clearly states Saul "immediately began to proclaim Jesus in the synagogues, saying, 'He is the Son of God.'" The people who heard Saul were amazed at what was already happening in his life, considering his previous lifestyle against those who claimed to know Jesus. Here's the most encouraging part, and a challenge to all of us: Acts 9:22 states, "But Saul kept increasing in strength and confounding the Jews who lived at Damascus by proving that this Jesus is the Christ."

Shortly after these events, some people attempted to kill Saul because of the message he was proclaiming about Jesus. But the opposition Saul was facing did not distract him from being obedient to God. After all these events, the Holy Spirit instructed the church at Antioch to "Set apart for Me

Barnabas and Saul for the work to which I have called them" (Acts 13:2). So Saul and Barnabas went together on a missionary trip and began to proclaim the Word of God, and it was clearly recorded in Acts 13:9, "But Saul, who was also known as Paul, filled with the Holy Spirit" began to boldly communicate the truth of God's Word to various people in various cities.

God also used Paul to heal a man in the city called Lystra. But some Jews came from another city and convinced the crowds to stone Paul, and they "dragged him out of the city, supposing him to be dead" (Acts 14:19), but he wasn't dead! God wasn't finished with him yet, and while the other disciples were standing around him, Paul got up. The very next day, in an amazing way, and only by the grace and strength of God, Paul and Barnabas went to another city and preached the gospel and made many disciples! God's grace is amazing, along with His power to change the lives of people and use them to glorify Himself. They also visited other cities where they had made many disciples, and God used them to strengthen "the souls of the disciples, encouraging them to continue in the faith, and saying, 'Through many tribulation we must enter the kingdom of God'" (Acts 14:22).

Paul continued to serve the Lord and preach the gospel to many others in many places. But even though Paul was loyal to the message of the gospel and the power of Christ, he and Silas were struck with many blows of a rod and throne into prison for the message they were proclaiming. But as God does with every situation, He had a purpose for what happened and a plan for what was about to happen. While they were in prison, it was "about midnight when Paul and Silas were praying and singing hymns of praise to God, and the prisoners were listening to them" (Acts 16:25). I've always thought if that were me, they would have been telling me, "Shut up!"

However, all of a sudden, there was a great earthquake and "immediately all the doors of the prison were opened and everyone's chains were unfastened" (Acts 16:26). As a result, when the jailor woke up, he pulled out his sword and was about to commit suicide because he was responsible to make sure none of those prisoners escaped, and if they did, he would be killed! But once again, God used His servant Paul to help someone. Acts 16:28 says "Paul cried out with a loud voice saying, 'Do not harm yourself, for we are all here!'" The jailor fell down before Paul and Silas, and then he responded with a question that you may be familiar with: "Sirs, what must I do to be saved?" God used Paul and Silas to provide us with an awesome and truthful statement: "Believe in the Lord Jesus Christ, and you will be saved, you and your household" (Acts 16:31). And that's exactly what happened in that jailor's life and in his household, and they were immediately baptized!

Once again, Paul's life clearly demonstrates *What God Can Do with an Idiot*. Paul lived the Word of God and proclaimed it to bring other people to a saving knowledge of Christ, and to encourage God's people to follow the Word of God and to think and act like Jesus so God can be gloried in our lives. But God still wasn't finished with Paul. The process continued as Paul went to Thessalonica, and God used him to persuade some people, "This Jesus whom I am proclaiming to you is the Christ" (Acts 17:3). But as usual, not everybody accepted that truth, and some responded in an ungodly way and "formed a mob and set the city in an uproar" (Acts 17:5). So God allowed the brethren of this city to immediately send Paul and Silas away by night to another city called Berea. Once again, God used Paul to preach the Word of God and make an impact on the lives of those who heard the message. In fact, it was said of the Bereans: "Now these were more noble minded than those in Thessalonica, for they received the word with great eagerness, examining the Scriptures daily to see whether these things were so. Therefore, many of them believed, along with a number of prominent Greek women and men" (Acts 17:11–12).

After Thessalonica, God led Paul to the city of Corinth, and Paul was "in the synagogue every Sabbath and trying to persuade Jews and Greeks" (Acts 18:4). It's interesting and challenging that when Silas and Timothy came to Corinth from another city, "Paul began devoting himself completely to the word, solemnly testifying to the Jews that Jesus was the

Christ" (Acts 18:5). But as usual, not everybody responded correctly to the Word of God, so when they resisted the truth and blasphemed the truth, Paul "shook out his garments and said to them, 'Your blood be on your own heads! I am clean. From now on I will go to the Gentiles'" (Acts 18:6). It is so encouraging to know what the Lord said to Paul after this happened. What the Lord told Paul should make all of us so thankful for a loving, tenderhearted, encouraging, and omnipotent God. Acts 18:9 clearly states, "And the Lord said to Paul in the night by a vision, 'Do not be afraid any longer, but go on speaking and do not be silent; for I am with you, and no man will attack you in order to harm you, for I have many people in this city." Paul ended up staying in Corinth for a year and six months, teaching the Word of God to those people.

God was still not finished with using the life of Paul! God led Paul to the city of Ephesus, and Paul re-baptized some of the believers who had misunderstood what baptism was all about. In addition to that action, Paul "laid his hand upon them, and the Holy Spirit came on them, and they began speaking with tongues and prophesying" (Acts 19:6). By now, we all probably see how God was using Paul's life in so many ways, and if God can do that with a man like Paul, who was an idiot named Saul, He can and will use us to bring glory to His name even though we sometimes make stupid decisions. God still pointed out to us how He was using Paul in Acts 19:11: "God was performing extraordinary miracles by the hand of Paul." God wasn't finished with him!

As God allowed Paul to continue on through Acts 20, Paul traveled to two other places called Macedonia and Greece. Paul taught and preached the Word of God to them and communicated his view of himself when he said to the elders of the church: "But I do not consider my life of any account as dear to myself, so that I may finish my course and the ministry which I received from the Lord Jesus, to testify solemnly of the gospel of the grace of God" (Acts 20:24).

God also used Paul to communicate a very important message to the elders of the church at Ephesus when Paul said to them: "For I did not shrink from declaring to you the whole purpose of God. Be on guard for yourselves and for all the flock, among which the Holy Spirit has made you oversees, to shepherd the church of God which He purchased with His own blood" (Acts 20:27–28). Paul went on to say to these elders of the church: "And now I commend you to God and to the word of His grace, which is able to build you up and to give you the inheritance among all those who are sanctified" (Acts 20:32). God used Paul as a tool for the truth to be spoken to many churches and to many people. Paul encouraged those who know the Lord to live their lives for the glory of God and not their own glory, and he challenged them to spread the gospel of Jesus Christ to the people around them—and to the whole world!

God still wasn't finished using this man named Paul who, before he became a Christian, had persecuted and even killed some of the people of God. And though he was not perfect even after he became a Christian, God used him as the second-most-prominent figure in the New Testament. However, even after he came to know the Lord, it's amazing the way Paul described himself as he was being inspired by the Holy Spirit to write the Word of God. Could you say these things about yourself?

> For I know that *nothing good dwells in me, that is, in my flesh*; for the willing is present in me, but the doing of the good is not. (Romans 7:18)

> We are *fools for Christ's sake*. (1 Corinthians 4:10)

> For I am *the least of the apostles, and not fit to be called an apostle*, because I persecuted the church of God. (1 Corinthians 15:9)

> To me, *the very least of all saints*, this grace was given, to preach to the Gentiles the unfathomable riches of Christ. (Ephesians 3:8)

> It is a trustworthy statement, deserving full acceptance, that Christ Jesus came into the world to save *sinners*, among whom *I am foremost of all*. (1 Timothy 1:15)

It's not about what you accomplished or the major results of your life because if it were not for God, you would not have accomplished *anything* in your life. Remember what Jesus said: "For apart from Me, you can do nothing" (John 15:5). Do you know what that Greek word *nothing* literally means? It literally means *nothing*—absolutely nothing! God took an idiot and used him to help a lot of people come to know Jesus Christ as their Lord and Savior, to help Christians to grow stronger in their knowledge of God and His Word, and to live by God's Word on a day-to-day and moment-by-moment lifestyle.

God used Paul to write thirteen books in the New Testament (maybe fourteen if Paul wrote the book of Hebrews). As you read a few of the most familiar verses the Holy Spirit inspired Paul to write, please take your time and think about yourself and the billions of people who have been influenced in many ways by these verses. Finally, please give some serious attention and be thankful to what God is trying to tell you about how you should think, and how you should act. God wants you to know how you can benefit from the encouraging words and commands God gave us through His servant Paul, who used to be Saul and is an amazing example of *What God Can Do with an Idiot*. Try to select one or two verses from each book that have impacted your life the most:

Romans

> For I am not ashamed of the gospel, for it is the power of God for salvation to everyone who believes, to the Jew first and also to the Greek. (Romans 1:16)

> For all have sinned and come short of the glory of God. (Romans 3:23)

But God demonstrated His own love toward us, in that while we were yet sinners, Christ dies for us. (Romans 5:8)

For the wages of sin is death, but the free gift of God is eternal life in Christ Jesus our Lord. (Romans 6:23)

And we know that God causes all things to work together for good to those who love God, to those who are called according to His purpose. (Romans 8:28)

For I am convinced that neither death, nor life, nor angels, nor principalities, nor things present, nor things to come, nor powers, nor heights, nor depth, nor any other created thing, will be able to separate us from the love of God which is in Christ Jesus our Lord. (Romans 8:38–39)

For "Whoever will call on the name of the Lord will be saved." (Romans 10:13)

So faith comes from hearing, and hearing by the word of Christ. (Romans 10:17)

Therefore, I urge you, brethren, by the mercies of God, to present your bodies a living and holy sacrifice, acceptable to God, which is your spiritual service of worship. And do not be conformed to this world, but be transformed by the renewing of your mind, so that you may prove what the will of God is, that which is good and acceptable and perfect. (Romans 12:1–2)

Never take your own revenge beloved, but leave room for the wrath of God, for it is written, "VENGEANCE IS MINE, I WILL REPAY," says the Lord. (Romans 12:19)

Do not be overcome by evil, but overcome evil with good. (Romans 12:21)

But put on the Lord Jesus Christ, and make no provision for the flesh in regard to its lust. (Romans 13:14)

So then each one of us will give an account of himself to God. (Romans 14:12)

1 Corinthians

For consider your calling, brethren, that there were not many wise according to the flesh, not many mighty, not many noble; but God has chosen the foolish things of the world to shame the wise, and God has chosen the weak things of the world to shame the things which are strong, and the base things of the world and the despised God has chosen, the things that are not, so that He may nullify the things that are, so that no man may boast before God. (1 Corinthians 1:26–29)

Or do you not know that the unrighteous will not inherit the kingdom of God? Do not be deceived: neither fornicators, nor idolaters, nor adulterers, nor effeminate, nor homosexuals, nor thieves, nor the covetous, nor drunkards, nor revilers, nor swindlers, will inherit the kingdom of God. Such were some of you; but you were justified in the name of the Lord Jesus Christ and in the Spirit of God. (1 Corinthians 6:9–12)

Or do you not know that your body is a temple of the Holy Spirit who is in you, whom you have from God, and that you are not your own? For you have been bought with a price: therefore glorify God in your body. (1 Corinthians 6:19–20)

No temptation has overtaken you but such is common to man; and God is faithful, who will not allow you to be tempted beyond what you are able, but with the temptation will provide the way of escape also, so that you will be able to endure it. (1 Corinthians 10:13)

Whether, then, you eat or drink or whatever you do, do all to the glory of God. (1 Corinthians 10:31)

But now faith, hope, love, abide these three; but the greatest of these is love. (1 Corinthians 13:13)

Therefore, my beloved brethren, be steadfast, immovable, always abounding in the work of the Lord, knowing that your toil is not in vain in the Lord. (1 Corinthians 15:58)

2 Corinthians

Blessed be the God and Father of our Lord Jesus Christ, the Father of mercies and God of all comfort Who comforts us in all our affliction so that we will be able to comfort those who are in any affliction with the comfort with which we ourselves are comforted by God. (2 Corinthians 1:3–4)

Therefore, we also have as our ambition, whether at home or absent, to be pleasing to Him. For we must all appear before the judgment seat of Christ so that each one may be recompensed for his deeds in the body, according to what he has done, whether good or bad. (2 Corinthians 5:9–10)

Therefore, we are ambassadors for Christ, as though God were making an appeal through us; we beg you on behalf of Christ, be reconciled to God. He made Him who knew no sin to be sin on our behalf, so that we might become the righteousness of God in Him. (2 Corinthians 5:20–21)

And He has said to me, "My grace is sufficient for you, for power is perfected in weakness." Most gladly, therefore, I will rather boast about my weaknesses, so that the power of Christ may dwell in me. (2 Corinthians 12:9)

Galatians

I have been crucified with Christ; and it is no longer I who live, but Christ live in me; and the life which I now live in the flesh I live by faith in the Son of God, who loved me and gave Himself for me. (Galatians 2:20)

But I say, walk by the Spirit and you will not carry out the deeds of the flesh. For the flesh sets its desire against the Spirit, and the Spirit against the flesh; for these are in opposition to one another, so that you may not do the things that you please. (Galatians 5:16–17)

Brethren, even if anyone is caught in any trespass, you who are spiritual, restore such a one in a spirit of gentleness; each one looking to yourself, so that you too will not be tempted. Bear one another's burdens, and thereby fulfill the law of Christ. (Galatians 6:1–2)

But may it never be that I would boast, except in the cross of our Lord Jesus Christ through which the world has been crucified to me, and I to the world. (Galatians 6:14)

Ephesians

For by grace you have been saved through faith; and that not of yourselves, it is the gift of God; not as a result of works, so that no one may boast. For we are His workmanship, created in Christ Jesus for good works which God prepared beforehand so that we would walk in them. (Ephesians 2:8–10)

Now to Him who is able to do far more abundantly beyond all that we ask or think, according to the power that works within us, to Him be the glory in the church and in Christ Jesus to all generations forever and ever. Amen. (Ephesians 3:20–21)

But speaking the truth in love, we are to grow up in all aspect into Him who is the head, even Christ. (Ephesians 4:15)

Be angry, and yet do not sin; do not let the sun go down on your anger. (Ephesians 4:26)

Let no unwholesome word proceed from your mouth, but only such a word as it good for edification according to the need of the moment, so that it will give grace to those who hear. (Ephesians 4:29)

Do not grieve the Holy Spirit of God, by whom you were sealed for the day of redemption. Let all bitterness and wrath and anger and clamor and slander be put away from you, along with all malice. Be kind to one another, tender hearted, forgiving each other, just as God in Christ has forgiven you. (Ephesians 4:30–32)

And do not get drunk with wine, for that is dissipation, but be filled with the Spirit. (Ephesians 5:18)

Speaking to one another in psalms, and hymns and spiritual songs, singing and making melody with your heart to the Lord; always giving thanks for all things in the name of our Lord Jesus Christ to God, even the Father. (Ephesians 5:19–20)

Wives be subject to your husbands, as to the Lord. (Ephesians 5:22)

Husbands love your wives just as Christ loved the church and gave Himself up for her. (Ephesians 5:25)

Children, obey your parents in the Lord, for this is right; Honor your father and mother (which is the first commandment with a promise), so that it may be well with you, and that you may live long on the earth. (Ephesians 6:1)

Finally, be strong I the Lord and in the strength of His might. Put on the full armor of God, so that you will be able to stand firm against the schemes of the devil. For our struggle is not against flesh and blood, but against the rulers, against the powers, against the world forces of the darkness, against the spiritual forces of wickedness in the heavenly places. Therefore, take up the full armor of God, so that you will be able to resist in the evil day, and having done everything, to stand firm. (Ephesians 6:10–13)

Philippians

For I am confident of this very thing that He who began a good work in you will perfect it until the day of Christ Jesus. (Philippians 1:6)

For to me to live is Christ and to die is gain. (Philippians 1:21)

For it is God who is at work in you, both to will and to work for His good pleasure. (Philippians 2:13)

That I may know Him and the power of His resurrection and the fellowship of His suffering, being conformed to His death. (Philippians 3:10)

Brethren, I do not regard myself as having laid hold of it yet; but one thing I do: forgetting what lies behind and reaching forward to what lies ahead, I press on toward the goal for the prize of the upward call of God in Christ Jesus. (Philippians 3:13–14)

Rejoice in the Lord always; again I say, rejoice! (Philippians 4:5)

Be anxious for nothing, but in everything by prayer and supplication with thanksgiving let your requests be made known to God. (Philippians 4:6)

Finally, brethren, whatever is true, whatever is honorable, whatever is right, whatever is pure, whatever is lovely, whatever is of good repute, if there is any excellence and if anything worthy of praise, dwell on these things. (Philippians 4:8)

I can do all things through Him who strengthens me. (Philippians 4:13)

And my God will supply all your needs according to His riches in glory in Christ Jesus. (Philippians 4:19)

Colossians

In whom we have redemption, the forgiveness of sins. (Colossians 1:14)

Therefore, as you have received Christ Jesus the Lord, so walk in Him. (Colossians 2:6)

Set you mind on the things above, not on the things that are on earth. (Colossians 3:2)

Let the word of Christ richly dwell within you, with all wisdom teaching and admonishing one another with psalms and hymns and spiritual songs, singing with thankfulness in your hearts to God. (Colossians 3:16)

Wives be subject to your husband, as is fitting in the Lord. Husbands, love your wives and do not be embittered against them. Children, be obedient to your parents in all things, for this is well-pleasing to the Lord. (Colossians 3:18–20)

Whatever you do, do your work heartily, as for the Lord rather than for men, knowing that from the Lord you will receive the reward of the inheritance. It is the Lord Christ whom you serve. (Colossians 3:23–24)

Let your speech always be with grace, as though seasoned with salt, so that you will know how you should respond to each person. (Colossians 4:6)

1 Thessalonians

For this is the will of God, your sanctification, that is, that you abstain from sexual immorality that each of you know how to possess his own vessel in sanctification and honor. (1 Thessalonians 4:3–4)

For God has not called us for the purpose of impurity, but in sanctification. So, he who rejects this is not rejecting man, but the God who gives His Holy Spirit to you. (1 Thessalonians 4:7–8)

But we do not want you to be uninformed, brethren, about those who are asleep, so that you will not grieve as do the rest who have no hope. For if we believe that Jesus died and rose again, even so God will bring with Him those who have fallen asleep in Jesus. For this we say to you by the word of the Lord, that we who are alive and remain until the coming of the Lord, will not precede those who have fallen asleep. For the Lord Himself will descend from heaven with a shout, with the voice of the archangel and with the trumpet of God, and the dead in Christ will rise first. Then we who are alive and remain will be caught up together with them in the clouds to meet the Lord in the air, and so we shall always be with the Lord. Therefore comfort one another with these words. (1 Thessalonians 4:13–18)

For you yourselves know full well that the day of the Lord will come like a thief in the night. (1 Thessalonians 5:2)

We urge you, brethren, admonish the unruly, encourage the fainthearted, help the weak, be patient with everyone. (1 Thessalonians 5:14)

Rejoice always. (1 Thessalonians 5:16)

Pray without ceasing. (1 Thessalonians 5:17)

In everything give thanks for this is God's will for you in Christ Jesus. (1 Thessalonians 5:18)

Faithful is He who calls you, and He also will bring it to pass. (1 Thessalonians 5:24)

2 Thessalonians

Now may our Lord Jesus Christ Himself and God our Father, who has loved us and given us eternal comfort and good hope by grace, comfort and strengthen your hearts in every good work and word. (2 Thessalonians 2:16–17)

But the Lord is faithful, and He will strengthen and protect you from the evil one. (2 Thessalonians 3:3)

If anyone does not obey our instruction in this letter, take special note of that person and do not associate with him, so that he will be put to shame. Yet do not regard him as an enemy, but admonish him as a brother. (2 Thessalonians 3:14–15)

1 Timothy

I thank Christ Jesus our Lord, who has strengthened me, because He considered me faithful, putting me into service. (1 Timothy 1:12)

It is a trustworthy statement; if any man aspires to the office of overseer, it is a fine work he desires to do. (1 Timothy 3:1)

On the other hand, discipline yourself for the purpose of godliness; for bodily discipline is only of little profit, but godliness is profitable for all things, since it holds promise for the present life and also for the life to come. (1 Timothy 4:7b–8)

But if anyone does not provide for his own, and especially for those of his household, he has denied the faith and is worse than an unbeliever. (1 Timothy 5:8)

Fight the good fight; take hold of the eternal life to which you were called, and you made the good confession in the presence of many witnesses. (1 Timothy 6:12)

2 Timothy

For this reason I also suffer these things, but I am not ashamed; for I know whom I have believed and I am convinced that He is able to guard what I have entrusted to Him until that day. (2 Timothy 1:12)

Be diligent to present yourself approved to God as a workman who does not need to be ashamed accurately handling the word of truth. (2 Timothy 2:15)

Nevertheless, the firm foundation of God stands, having this seal, "The Lord knows those who are His" and, "Everyone who names the name of the Lord is to abstain from wickedness." (2 Timothy 2:19)

Therefore, if anyone cleanses himself from this things, he will be a vessel for honor, sanctified, useful to the Master, prepared for every good work. (2 Timothy 2:21)

Now flee from youthful lusts and purse righteousness, faith, love, and peace, with those who call on the Lord from a pure heart. (2 Timothy 2:22)

The Lord's bond-servant must not be quarrelsome, but be kind to all, able to teach, patient when wronged, with gentleness correcting those who are in opposition, if perhaps God may grant them repentance leading to the knowledge of the truth, and they may come to their senses and escape from the snare of the devil, having been held captive by him to do his will. (2 Timothy 2:25–26)

Indeed, all who desire to live godly in Christ Jesus will be persecuted. (2 Timothy 3:12)

All Scripture is inspired by God and profitable for teaching, for reproof, for correction, for training in righteousness; so that the man of God may be adequate, equipped for every good work. (2 Timothy 3:16–17)

In the future there is laid up for me the crown of righteousness, which the Lord the righteous Judge, will award to me on that day; and not only to me, but also to all who have loved His appearing. (2 Timothy 4:8)

But the Lord stood with me and strengthened me, so that through me the proclamation might be fully accomplished, and that all the Gentiles might hear; and I was rescued out of the lion's mouth. The Lord will rescue me from every evil deed, and will bring me safely to His heavenly kingdom; to him be the glory forever and ever. Amen. (2 Timothy 4:17–18)

Titus

To the pure, all things are pure; but to those who are defiled and unbelieving, nothing is pure, but both their mind and their conscience are defiled. They profess to know God, but by their deed they deny Him, being detestable and disobedient and worthless for any good deed. (Titus 1:15–16)

For the grace of God has appeared, bringing salvation to all men, instructing us to deny ungodliness and worldly desires and to live sensibly, righteously and godly in the present age, looking for the blessed hope and the appearing of the glory of our great God and Savior, Christ Jesus, who gave Himself for us to redeem us from every lawless deed, and to purify for Himself a people for His own possession, zealous for good deeds. (Titus 2:11–14)

Philemon

I thank my God always, making mention of you in my prayers. (Philemon 1:4)

Hebrews

Therefore, since we have a great high priest who has passed through the heavens, Jesus the Son of God, let us hold fast our confessions. For we do not have a high priest who cannot sympathize with our weaknesses, but One who has been temped in all things as we are yet without sin. Therefore let us draw near with confidence to the throne of grace so that we may receive mercy and find grace to help in time of need. (Hebrews 4:14–16)

And let us consider how to stimulate one another to love and good deeds, not forsaking our own assembling together, as is the habit of some, but encouraging one another; and all the more as you see the day drawing near. (Hebrews 10:24–25)

And without faith it is impossible to please Him, for he who comes to God must believer that He is and that He is a rewarder of those who seek Him. (Hebrews 11:6)

Therefore, since we have so great a cloud of witnesses surrounding us, let us also lay aside every encumbrance and the sin which so easily entangles us, and let us run with endurance the race that is set before us. Fixing our eyes on Jesus, the author and perfecter of faith, who for the joy set before Him endured the cross, despising the shame, and has sat down at the right hand of the throne of God. For consider Him who has endured such hostility by sinners against Himself, so that you will not grow weary and lose heart. (Hebrews 12:1–?)

Jesus Christ is the same yesterday and today and forever. (Hebrews 13:8)

Obey your leaders and submit to them, for they keep watch over your souls as those who will give an account. Let them do this with joy and not with grief, for this would be unprofitable for you. (Hebrews 13:17)

I want to close this chapter with a key passage the Holy Spirit inspired Paul to write in Galatians 1:22–24: "I was still unknown by sight to the churches of Judea which were in Christ; but only, they kept hearing, "He who once persecuted us is now preaching the faith which he once tried to destroy." And they were glorifying God because of me." That's an awesome example of *What God Can Do with an Idiot*! What does God want to do with you? Study His Word as you pray, and ask Him, and He will tell you!

Here are my final questions: How have you allowed God to use an idiot like Paul to make an impact on your life? Has his testimony encouraged you to fight the good fight, and to finish your course, and to keep the faith? Are you encouraged that God can take a man who was killing Christians and use that person to bring glory to His name and influence trillions of people? Are you "putting off the old man" and "putting on the new man" so you can grow to think and act more like Christ and therefore glorify God?

Here's my point: If God can use somebody like Saul to become Paul, then what is God able to do with *you* if you will listen to what God tells you? Don't be a *stupid idiot;* submit to God and obey His Word, and ask Him to help you to love Him with all of your heart, and to serve Him everyday of your life for His glory! Remember, one of these days you'll see Jesus face-to-face! What do you want to hear Him tell you? I'm sure you want Him to say, "Well done, good and faithful slave. You were faithful with a few things, I will put you in charge of many things; enter into the joy of your master" (Matthew 25:21).

CHAPTER 15

We're All Idiots!

What God Can Do with People Like Us!

I realize that you still may be struggling with the title of this book, and even now more specifically the title of this chapter. If that's the case, then you just proved my point—you're an idiot! But I want you to know, I'll be the first to admit I'm an idiot. Somebody put the following statement on a Facebook post, and I thought it would be good to use in this chapter: *"To be old and wise, you first must be young and stupid. When do you know you've crossed that line?"* I know I've crossed that line, and I'm thankful there's evidence in my life that reveals *What God Can Do with an Idiot*. God used a lot of other idiots in my life to help me take a lot of steps of spiritual growth and seek to live my life to glorify God. And even though there are times when I've failed terribly, I'm holding to the truth that, "If we confess our sins, He is faithful and righteous to forgive us our sins and to cleanse us from all unrighteousness" (1 John 1:9). I can answer that Facebook question because I know when I crossed that line.

As you've seen in the previous chapters, just because somebody else crosses the line of stupidity doesn't mean you won't be an idiot the rest of your life, or you will never make a stupid decision. You could probably give some examples of some stupid decisions you've made, and if you don't think you have any, I'm sure your family and friends probably could give a few examples about you! We can avoid being idiots by choosing to obey the Word of God every day and in every situation we face. Even though we have been forgiven of our sin because we are washed in the blood of Lamb and have been legally declared righteous on the account books of heaven, we still have to admit that we're still not perfect. We need to grow to think and act more like Christ so we can bring glory to God. We don't *have* to sin, but we still *choose* to sin because the curse of sin, which affects our bodies and our ability to think and reason, is not yet removed from our lives. It won't be removed until Jesus comes and takes us back to heaven, or we die and enter into His presence in heaven. However, Paul wrote in Ephesians 4:22–24 about how a person can change and grow: "In reference to your former manner of life, you lay aside the old self, which is being corrupted in accordance with the lusts of deceit, and that you be renewed in the spirit of your mind, and put on the new self, which in the likeness of God has been created in righteousness and holiness of the truth." If we're growing spiritually and thinking like Christ, we will bring more glory to God because we will make godly decisions, and we will sin less. We'll be smarter and therefore, less stupid!

You probably know that someday when Christians get to heaven, the curse of sin will be removed, and we won't think or act like an idiot ever again because we will finally be "conformed to the image of Christ" (Romans 8:29). This chapter encourages people who will admit that they know Jesus as their Savor and Lord, but they are still not perfect, so that makes them an idiot; but they also realize they are not the only idiots in this life. God is with us, but there are other idiots all around us. So, the questions are: Are we growing to think and act more like Christ so we can glorify God? Are we obedient to God's Word? How quickly are we going to admit we've disobeyed God's Word and sinned against Him and somebody else? Are we going to 'put off' the old man and 'put on' the new man so

WE'RE ALL IDIOTS!

we can take some steps of growth? There are also situations where God clearly stated what He wanted us to do, but we don't want to do it, so we don't do it. That's exactly what happened in Jonah's situation. That kind of response is labeled as rebellion, disobedience, a sinful choice, and yes … a stupid choice, and whoever makes that choice is an idiot! But as we saw in the life of Jonah, when we repent and listen to God, He can still use us.

This chapter is also challenging the kind of person who would say, "I'm not an idiot! How dare you call me something like that? I've been wise and made godly choices. Look at my life and all the blessings from God that I'm enjoying. Look at the results of all I've done and accomplished because of my hard work and the way I've handled things." A person who would think that way and talk that way is not a smart and humble person. Instead, that individual is stupid and proud. A smart person and a godly person humbles himself/herself and admits he/she is an idiot and will listen to what the Holy Spirit inspired an idiot named Peter to write: "And all of you, clothe yourselves with humility toward one another, for God is opposed to the proud, but gives grace to the humble" (1 Peter 5:5). So let's be smart and humble so we can seriously think about how we are real idiots sometimes. We desperately need God's help to reveal our idiocy so we can grow and change to think and act more like Jesus Christ, our Savior and Lord, who is the *only* sinless person and *perfectly* humble person and completely *wise* person who walked on this earth when He came to die for our sin. We need to think and act like Him if we are going to please God and give evidence of our salvation and make a godly impact on the lives of others.

When's the last time you made a stupid decision? Was it a few minutes ago, earlier today, yesterday, or a couple of days ago? I don't think we need to go any further back. You could probably give an example of a stupid decision you made last week, last month, last year, a couple of years ago, or a long time ago. Hopefully, it's a lesson God helped you to learn, and you're not making the same stupid decision over and over again. But even if a person is a Christian, that person is not perfect. While the blood of Jesus Christ has washed away our sin, and we are forgiven of our sin and washed "whiter than snow" (Psalm 51), we all still make sinful choices sometimes. But if we keep sinning the same way over and over again and show no evidence of repentance and spiritual growth, we better question if we truly know Christ. Yes, we're all idiots. However, we're more than idiots if we keep sinning over and over again in the same way and don't repent or confess our sin to God and the appropriate people, and there is no spiritual change or growth in our life. God warns us that if we continually practice sin and don't repent, then we are not born of God (1 John 5:18). But even if you are a child of God, you're still not perfect, and you need to keep growing spiritually in all areas of your life and your relationship with the Lord and with other people. If you've sinned, then be humble and repent and confess your sin to God and the appropriate people, and grow to think and act more like Christ. If someone has sinned against you, God commands you to forgive that person. If you won't forgive someone of his or her sin, then Jesus said that your Father will not forgive you of your sin (Matthew 6:15).

The people we've studied in the previous chapters were idiots, but they learned from it and didn't keep sinning in the same way for the rest of their lives. They were not perfect, so they were still idiots, but they kept growing and learning from the stupid choices they made along the way of life. Think about how David responded in Psalm 51 to the sins he committed! No wonder he was later called "a man after God's own heart." Think about how Peter responded when the rooster crowed, and Jesus looked at him. Peter "went out and wept bitterly." Jesus had already told him, "When you've turned back, strengthen your brothers," and that's exactly what Peter did.

We need to keep in mind that God knows everything that happens in our lives and everything that is going to happen. The Holy Spirit inspired David to write: "O God, thou knowest my foolishness; and my sins are not hid from thee" (Psalm 69:5 KJV). However, being a God of grace (giving us what we don't deserve) and mercy (withholding what we do deserve), He can still use us in a lot of different ways to bring glory to His name—even through the life of idiots like you and me! Someone once told me, "The first step in solving a problem is to realize you have one!" Therefore, after you admit you're an idiot, the next step is to ask God's forgiveness, and the forgiveness of those whom we've sinned against, for being so stupid and not following what God said in His Word to do or not to do. Then we need to follow Ephesians 4:22–24 and "lay aside the old self, which is being corrupted in accordance with the lust of deceit" and "be renewed in the spirit of your mind" (which means to change our thinking) and then "put on the new self, which in the likeness of God has been created in righteousness and holiness of the truth." This process is known as progressive sanctification, which is the process of growing and changing in our thinking and our actions—ultimately, to think and act like Christ so we can bring glory to God.

The idiot who's writing this book grew up in a Christian home and went to church on a regular basis. When I was thirteen years old, I started growing and smoking marijuana. As my life progressed, my use of drugs and alcohol rapidly increased to dangerous levels on many occasions. I was using drugs and selling drugs, and I was getting drunk with alcohol. I got in a lot physical fights, and I did a lot of wrong things and stupid things. But when I turned sixteen years old and got my driver's license, I went with my cousin, Rhonella Dutton, to a basketball game at the Christian school she attended in Decatur, Alabama. While at the game, I met a girl who used to go to the church my family attended. Yes, I went to church with my family every Sunday, but that doesn't make a person a Christian.

A couple days later, I called that girl and asked her out for a date. However, she told me no! But she loved the Lord and loved people, so she spoke the truth in a loving way and told me why she said no to a date: "Mark, I know all about your drug abuse and the trouble you've been in.

WHAT GOD CAN DO WITH AN IDIOT

Your cousin has requested prayer for you many times, and my dad won't let me date you because he's seen you drunk at football games. And besides, based on your life, I don't think you are a Christian, so I don't think God wants me to date you." You know what? She was right! I thanked her for being honest with me and speaking kindly to me, then I said good-bye, and I hung up the phone. That's when I got down on my knees, and I prayed to the Lord and said, "Lord, I thought I was a Christian. But knowing all the things I've been doing, I think Becky is right. I don't think I am a Christian. Lord, I believe Jesus died on the cross and shed His blood to save me from my sin, and He rose from the dead so He could offer me eternal life. Lord, if I am a Christian, then please forgive me and help me to change; if I'm not a Christian, then I admit that I'm a sinner, and would You please forgive me and cleanse me from my sin? I'm asking Jesus to be my Lord and Savior." Well guess what? January 6, 1977 is the day I became a Christian because God forgave me of my sin, and Jesus became my Savior and Lord, and my life changed immediately and drastically!

One month later, I left my public school and started attending the Christian school my cousin attended. I was so shocked by the loving way the students and teachers in that Christian school accepted me. They treated me like a brother they had known and loved for a long time. God especially used a young man named Vann Spears who was in my class and befriended me, encouraged me, challenged me, and helped me to grow as a Christian. Vann, along with many others, demonstrated godly love to his brother in Christ and to his friend.

Because of Vann and other godly and friendly people at that school, God revealed a huge lesson to me early in my Christian life. The lesson was that people who don't show love to an unsaved person, or to a fellow brother or sister in Christ, are violating the second-greatest commandment to "love your neighbor as yourself" (Matthew 22:39). God is *not* pleased with a person's unloving and sinful choices that reveal a person to be a super-idiot on steroids! If that's the way a person treats other people, then that person needs to ask God's forgiveness and ask God for help to change and grow to think and act like Christ "who knew no sin to be sin on our behalf, so that we might become the righteousness of God in Him" (2 Corinthians 5:21), and to whom God the Father said, "This is my beloved Son, in whom I am well pleased" (Matthew 3:16). If we will be like Christ, God will be pleased with us, and if we don't think and act like Christ, God will not be pleased with us! God used that idiot named Paul to tell this truth: "Be diligent to present yourself to God as a workman who does not need to be ashamed, accurately handling the word of truth" (2 Timothy 2:15). That last phrase means to properly understand the word of truth, to proclaim it, and most importantly, to obey it and lovingly help others to grow in their spiritual lives as we share "the word of truth" with them.

Since "We Are All Idiots" all of us should read, think about, and most importantly, put into practice the truth God revealed to us about His love for us in Romans 8:31–39:

> What then shall we say to these things? If God is for us, who is against us? He who did not spare His own Son, but delivered Him over for us all, how will He not also with Him freely give us all things? Who will bring a charge against God's elect? God is the one who justifies; who is the one who condemns? Christ Jesus is He who died, yes, rather who was raised, who is at the right hand of God, who also intercedes for us. Who will separate us from the love of Christ? Will tribulation, or distress, or persecution, or famine, or nakedness, or peril, or sword? Just as it is written, "For Your sake we are being put to death all day long; We were considered as sheep to be slaughtered." But in all these things we overwhelmingly conquer through Him who loved us. For I am convinced that neither death, nor life, nor angels, nor principalities, nor things present, nor things to come,

nor powers, nor height, nor depth, nor any other created thing, will be able to separate us from the love of God, which is in Christ Jesus our Lord.

As you think about God's love for you, think about these questions and ask them for yourself regarding your love for Him and your love for others:

1) Do I believe God loves me no matter how big of an idiot I am?
2) Do I love God and seek to be growing in my love for Him and my love for others?
3) Do I try to keep His commandments to demonstrate my love for Him?
4) Do I seek to glorify (lit. to give the right opinion) Him and not myself?
5) Do I show God's love to others who have sinned against me or have sinned against someone else?
6) Do I scorn those who have sinned against me and tell them to leave me alone and don't talk to me again?
7) Do I violate Proverbs 18:13 by making false accusations about someone without getting all the facts?
8) Do I consider what our church would be like if everybody loved God and loved others the same way I do?
9) Do I consider what our church would be like if everybody responded to people or situations the way I do?
10) Do I take steps of growth in my love for God and love for others and demonstrate that love?
11) Do I really want other people to treat me the same way I'm treating them?
12) Do I realize someday I will stand face to face with Jesus when He judges my life at the judgment seat of Christ?

I really appreciate and agree with what Charles Spurgeon said: "My faith rests not upon what I am, or shall be, or feel, or know, but in what

Christ is, in what He has done, and what He is now doing for me."[1] Whatever Christ is doing in our lives, He's doing it because He loves us. What He is doing will bring glory to Him in ways we probably don't fully understand! Even though we don't always understand what He's doing or not doing, or why He's doing it or not letting it happen, we need to remember what God told us: "For My thoughts are not your thoughts, nor are your ways My ways," declares the Lord. "For as the heavens are higher than the earth, so are My ways higher than your ways and My thoughts than your thoughts" (Isaiah 55:8–9).

Honestly, the title "We're All Idiots" refers primarily to the most sinful, selfish, stupid, ignorant, proud, deceiver, and liar that has ever existed and will always be the most wicked, corrupt, ungodly, and sinful example of an idiot. God created this angel, like all the other angels in the heavens, for the purpose of worshiping and glorifying God. This angel is known as Lucifer, also known as Satan, and as the Devil. He wants us to think and act like we are smarter than God so we don't have to listen to what the Word of God says, and we sure don't have to obey God's Word because God is not our final authority—nobody is! Satan wants us to think we can do whatever we want to do, and whatever we do or don't do is perfect! He wants us to think that everybody ought to think and act like we do. Satan wants us to put our focus on results and what we accomplish rather than on relationships and demonstrating godly love to people. Satan lies and tries to deceive us by telling us even if we do something wrong, we won't face the consequences. Satan lies and tries to deceive people and often succeeds in convincing people that there is no God, there is no heaven, and there is no hell, so what are you worried about? It's interesting—the man who was called the Beloved Apostle (referring to John) wrote the words Jesus spoke to a group of Jews. Jesus was referring to Satan in John 8:44: "You are of your father the devil, and you want to do the desires of your father. He was a murderer from the beginning, and does not stand in the truth

---

[1] Facebook: Bayside Chapel Youth Group, November 9, 2014.

because there is not truth in him. Whenever he speaks a lie, he speaks from his own nature, for he is a liar, and the Father of Lies." Satan is the most stupid idiot of all idiots, and someday he will face the consequences of his stupid thinking and stupid choices when he is cast into the fires of Hell where he will burn and suffer for eternity!

In addition to what John was inspired to write, the Holy Spirit also inspired the prophet Isaiah to write these words in the Old Testament in Isaiah 14:12–15: "How you have fallen from heaven, O star of the morning, son of the dawn! You have been cut down to the earth, You who have weakened the nations! But you said in your heart, 'I will ascend to heaven; I will raise my throne above the stars of God, and I will sit on the mount of assembly in the recesses of the north. I will ascend above the heights of the clouds; I will make myself like the Most High.' Nevertheless you will be thrust down to Sheol, to the recesses of the pit." *Sheol* is known as hell or the lake of fire and the bottomless pit! That's where Satan, the "liar and Father of lies," will spend eternity suffering and being tortured by the darkness, falling in the bottomless pit, and the flames of fire that will never be quenched!

It's clear that Satan hates God the Father, God the Son, and God the Holy Spirit. He also hates the church who are God's chosen people and purchased with the blood of Christ. Satan wants to bring strife and division to the Church to break up the body of Christ. Satan wants to lead the Church down a path of *pride* by trying to get everyone to think, "*Everything we do is exactly what God wants us to do*" or "*Everything we say, and all the advice and counsel we give, is exactly what God would say and exactly the advice and counsel God would give.*" If that's the way a person or a church is thinking, then nobody will listen to God's Word anymore because they'll just listen to each other's prideful opinions and thoughts, and will reveal that sin in a lot of different ways that will rob God of His glory and will be hurtful and do damage to people and their relationship with others. Satan hates Christians, and he wants to destroy our lives, our marriages, our families, our friendships, our ministries, and our testimony to others so we cannot be "the salt of the earth" or "the light of the world" as God intended for us be (Matthew 5:13–16).

Guess what? Satan not only hates God, he also hates the Word of God because it reveals Satan's character and reminds him of his future that God clearly and boldly communicates. Satan knows someday God will cast him into the lake of fire…forever, along with all his demons, and anyone whose name is not found written in the Lamb's Book of life! Do you know what that word *forever* literally means? It means *forever*! And that "lake of fire" is also called hell "where their worm does not die, and the fire is not quenched" (Mark 9:43–48). Satan wants to take as many people to hell as he possibly can, so that's why he wants to destroy the life of a Christian. The destruction of a Christian's life can destroy a person's testimony to the point that an unsaved person would not ever listen to a professing Christian who is trying to share the Gospel with him or her and lead him or her to a saving knowledge of the Lord Jesus Christ! Satan also hates and wants to destroy a Christian's marriage because a marriage is a picture of Christ's love for the church. Satan also wants to destroy a Christian's family, ministry, and friendships. With so much at stake, we're stupid if we avoid, ignore, or minimize God's instruction to us in Ephesians 6:10–11: "Finally, be strong in the Lord and in the strength of His might. Put on the full armor of God, so that you will be able to stand firm against the schemes of the devil." If we don't fight back with God's help and God's armor, Satan will win many battles, and there will be lots of consequences because we are idiots! James was inspired by the Holy Spirit to write: "Submit therefore to God. Resist the devil, and he will flee from you" (James 4:7). If we don't submit and resist, we're *idiots*!

While God inspired others to write His Word, He wants us to obey His Word. Jesus said, "If you love Me, you will keep my commandments" (John 14:15). How could anybody make a more simple statement than what Jesus said? If we love Him, we will obey His commands. If we don't love Him, then we won't obey His commands. Our disobedience reveals that we are selfish, proud, stubborn, lazy, and temporal-minded instead of eternal-minded. Most of all, we'll be stupid idiots (which does not mean someone could be a 'smart idiot'). I'm trying to communicate that there are various levels of *idiocy*. As you know, "We're All Idiots," but there are also various consequences for various acts of stupidity. Think about the warning Paul wrote in Galatians 6:3: "For if anyone thinks he is something when he is nothing, he deceive himself." Galatians 6:8 clearly states, "For the one who sows to his own flesh will from the flesh reap corruption, but the one who sows to the Spirit will from the Spirit read eternal life."

Part of sowing to the Spirit, and our obedience to His commands, is to read, study, memorize, and meditate on His Word, and to proclaim His Word to people who are lost and going to hell if they don't hear the gospel and believe it! Jesus also wants us to share the truth of His Word with our brothers or sisters in Christ to help them make the right decision *before* they sin, and to help them know what to do *after* they have sinned and are about to face the consequences of their disobedience that God has already revealed or is about to reveal to them. In the process of God using one Idiot to help another Idiot, you can share the verse in Proverbs 12:1: "Whoever loves discipline loves knowledge, but he who hates reproof is *stupid.*"

Of course, that truth is to be applied to the husband and to the wife, to the parent and to the children, to the pastor and to the church member, to the counselor and to the counselee, to the employer and to the employee, to the teacher and to the student, and to you and to your friends! Ask God to help you be a person who "loves discipline and knowledge" so you won't hate reproof and be *stupid*, even though "We're All Idiots" because we're not perfect. We all need to remember what the Holy Spirit inspired the man who denied Christ three times while cursing and swearing to later write: "But grow in grace and in the knowledge of our Lord and Savior, Jesus Christ" (2 Peter 3:18). Are you growing?

If I could say one thing about all of us, it would be, "We're all idiots!"

Nobody is perfect, and nobody is always right. When—not if, but *when*—we think we are always right and nobody is as right as we are and look at all the results of all the specific choices we've made, then we are bigger idiots than anybody could imagine, and we just might be on the edge of God disciplining us for our pride and self-righteousness. We can take credit for what we've accomplished, or we can brag about it and say to others, "Look how God has blessed *me* so much—look at the all the results I've accomplished!" If that's the person's attitude, then he or she is not only an idiot, but that person has another problem called pride, which is the root of being an idiot. God warns us, "Pride goes before destruction, and a haughty spirit before stumbling" (Proverbs 16:18). The destruction and stumbling come because God hates pride. When we start bragging, we need to remember what Jesus said: "for apart from Me, you can do nothing" (John 15:5). Do you remember what that Greek word *nothing* means? It means *nothing*! We cannot do *anything* without the help of Jesus. When I was a freshman in college, one of my teachers quoted that verse and really emphasized the word *nothing*. He was shouting and telling us that the word *nothing* means *absolutely nothing*! One of my friends raised his hand and asked our teacher, "Do you mean that I can't even go to the bathroom without Jesus?" Our teacher responded with a *shouting* voice, "Absolutely, because if your kidneys and intestines do not function the way God designed them to function, then *you ... will ... die!*" About two hundred students laughed for a long time because he was right, and I've never forgotten what he said. Often times I've reminded myself, or someone else, of that truth. There have been times when I didn't remind myself of that truth, and I was an idiot for thinking I could do it without Jesus!

We have to keep in mind that nobody else but Jesus will make the final judgments on a person's life. One day each Christian will stand before Him at the judgment seat of Christ. Paul was inspired to write this important truth in 2 Corinthians 5:9–10: "Therefore we also have as our ambition, whether at home or absent, to be pleasing to Him. For we must all appear before the judgment seat of Christ, so that each one may recompensed for his deeds in the body, according to what he has done, whether good or bad." Christ will tell us about what we've done or not done. He will be the One who rightly evaluates the results we are so quick to brag about to draw attention to ourselves so people will notice our gifts and abilities and see what we've been able to accomplish. Well, that's called *pride* and *boasting*. God doesn't tolerate either one of those, and He surely doesn't reward it! Paul was inspired to write a letter to the church at Corinth who needed to hear this warning. He wrote in 1 Corinthians 3:10–15:

> According to the grace of God which was given to me, like a wise master builder I laid a foundation, and another is building on it. But each man must be careful how he builds on it. For no man can lay a foundation other than the one which is laid, which is Jesus Christ. Now if any man builds on the foundation with gold, silver, precious stones, wood, hay, straw, each man's work will become evident; for the day will show it because it is to be revealed with fire, and the fire itself will test the quality of each man's work. If any man's work which he has built on it remains, he will receive a reward. If any man's work is burned up, he will suffer loss; but he himself will be saved, yet so as through fire.

God can use us to accomplish His will in our lives and to help others accomplish His will in their lives, even though sometimes we are idiots, and we make decisions that have a negative impact on the whole process or a negative impact on the lives of those involved in the process. But if we ask God to forgive us, guess what? He promised He would do it! He confirmed that truth in one of the most encouraging passages in God's

Word. God gives us His promise in 1 John 1:9: "If we confess our sin, He is faithful and righteous to forgive us our sins and to cleanse us from all unrighteousness." In response, we should say to the Lord:

> "Lord, I was sinful when I _____ (fill in the blank), and I was stupid and selfish and did not obey You! Will You please forgive me and help me to face the consequences of my sinful choice(s) and to learn from my sinful choice(s) so I won't do that again? Will You help me to restore my relationship with You? Will you help me to restore my relationship with the person or the persons I have offended? Will you work in that person's heart or the heart of those people I've sinned against and bring each one to the place where they will forgive me and restore our relationship? Even if there is a person or persons who will not forgive me, nor seek to restore my relationship with them, I know You will forgive me and restore our relationship so You can be glorified, and I can 'press on' in my life and ministry to bring more glory to you as you demonstrate *What God Can Do with an Idiot*."

It's encouraging to know that God's amazing grace, along with His omniscience (all-knowing) and His omnipotence (all-powerful) can overcome our stupidity and help us put the pieces of our lives back together with Him and the people in our lives. This can be done in a way that He will be glorified for what is accomplished in our lives as we continue to be tools in the hand of the Redeemer and 'press on' till Jesus returns at the Rapture of the church, or He stops our earthly life and takes us home to heaven.

When (not if) we do things wrong, we are double idiots if we're not willing to *repent* (which literally means to have a change of the mind) and to *confess* (which literally means to say that same thing God would say) and to *restore* (which literally means to mend the net or to set the bone) our relationships with those we have offended—which includes God Himself and any other person involved in our stupid and sinful choices! Please don't be an idiot right now and be thinking about the person who offended you and needs to do all these things we just mentioned! If *we* want to avoid being an idiot, then *we* need to think about *our* sin and how stupid *we* have been and how *we* have offended God, or another person, or other persons. We need to consider how *we* need to repent, confess, and restore our relationships with God and with that person or those other people *we've* sinned against. Jesus made it very clear how this process is to take place when He said in Matthew 7:5, "You hypocrite, first take the log out of your own eye, and then you will see clearly to take the speck out of your brother's eye."

It's comforting and motivating to know when God forgives us, He doesn't keep bringing it up against us over and over again. When He forgives us, it's done, and we are forgiven because He loves us. And even though there may be consequences to the choices we've made, God will help us to restore (which means to mend the net or set the bone that was broken) our relationship with Him and our relationship with those we've offended. But God may have to help the people we've offended to grant our forgiveness and restore their relationship with us!

Sometimes our idiocy is revealed in our sinful choices but also revealed in our unforgiving spirit, our bitterness toward someone who offended us, or our attempts in an unbiblical way to punish that person who sinned against us. One of the biggest attempts to punish others is to ignore them, stay away from them, and not communicate or discuss anything with them. God doesn't do that with us, so why would we do it? The answer is simple: We're All Idiots! We all have to remember what Jesus said: "But if you do not forgive others, then your Father will not forgive your transgressions" (Matthew 6:15). What is it about that promise that we don't understand? God makes it clear that if we want forgiveness, we have to forgive. Jesus commanded us to "love one another even as I have loved you" (John 13:34). If we don't love each other like Jesus loves us, then we are idiots. We also are robbing God of His glory because we are not demonstrating His love to others the way He has demonstrated His love to us. A detailed description of God's love is given to us in 1 Corinthians 13, and an eternal demonstration of God's love for us is given in John 3:16. There is no reason for us not to love God, and therefore keep His commandments. There is no reason for us not to love other people even though they're idiots sometime, like us!

I would strongly suggest, if you haven't already done it, that you memorize the following verses to help you make wise decisions every day that will bring glory to God and allow God to use you as tool in His hand to accomplish His will for your life and the lives of others:

> Therefore, since we have so great a cloud of witnesses surrounding us, let us also *lay aside* every encumbrance and the sin which so easily entangles us, and let us *run with endurance* the race that is set before us, *fixing our eyes on Jesus*, the author and perfecter of faith, who for the joy set before Him endured the cross, despising the shame, and has sat down at the right hand of the throne of God. For *consider Him* who has endured such hostility by sinners against Himself, *so that you will not grow weary and lose heart.* (Hebrews 12:1–4)

Since "We're All Idiots" and we can't really trust ourselves, we need to ask ourselves a couple of questions that might help us to take some steps of growth away from our stupidity. Think about the following questions:

1. Why would we disobey the God:
- Who created the heavens and the earth with the word of His mouth in six literal twenty-four-hour days?
- Who holds the universe in the palm of His hand?

- Who knows the stars by names?
- Who created man from the dust of the ground and breathed into him the breath of life?
- Who flooded the earth in forty days, but saved Noah's family and some creatures?
- Who parted the Red Sea and the Jordan River and killed all the soldiers who were chasing God's chosen people?
- Who brought down the walls of Jericho?
- Who used a wise man to save the life of a little baby?
- Who helped a young man named David to kill a giant and cut off his head?
- Who helped a man named Job get through the fiery trials of his life?
- Who saved Daniel from being killed and eaten in the lion's den?
- Who saved three men from the fiery furnace and they didn't even smell like smoke when they came out?
- Who put a man in the belly of a whale but made the whale spit him back out?

2. **Why would we not follow the footstep of Jesus:**
   - Who was born of a virgin?
   - Who made the blind to see, the deaf to hear, and the lame to walk?
   - Who raised Lazarus from the dead?
   - Who walked on water?
   - Who said, "Peace, be still" and calmed the raging sea?
   - Who turned the water into wine?
   - Who knew one of His disciples would curse and swear and deny Him three times but He still loved that disciple?
   - Who would experience His suffering while His twelve disciples forsook Him and fled?
   - Who allowed His eyes to be covered so He would not know when He was going to be struck by a Roman soldier who would put all his weight behind a curled fist when the solder hit Him?

- Who allowed Himself to be beaten with a whip that caused blood to flow out of His body?
- Who allowed a crown of thorns to be jammed onto His head?
- Who allowed nails to be driven into His hands and feet?
- Who was falsely judged, but He never opened His mouth?
- Who "became sin for us who knew no sin that we might be made the righteousness of God in Him"?
- Who while on the cross cried, "My God, My God, why have You forsaken me?"
- Who prayed while He was dying on the cross, "Father, forgive them because they do not know what they are doing"?
- Who said on the cross, "It is finished," which is only one Greek word that literally means a past action with ongoing continuous results?
- Who rose from the dead three days after He died to give us eternal life?
- Who saved us from a place called hell where "the worm does not die and the fire is not quenched"?
- Who is coming again to set up His millennial kingdom?
- Who will reward us according to our work for Him?
- Who will cast everybody into hell whose name is not written in the Lamb's Book of Life?
- Who will recreate the heavens and the earth in one day with the word of His mouth?
- Who will spend eternity with us providing us a mansion and streets of gold?
- Who promised that He would return to bring us to heaven?
- Who promised He would never leave us nor forsake us?
- Who promised that nothing can separate us from the love of God which is in Christ Jesus?
- Who one day will be our final judge at the judgment seat of Christ?

- Who will finally cast Satan—the liar, and the father of lies, and the deceiver—into hell forever, where the worm does not die and the fire is not quenched?
- Who will cast all the demons of Satan into hell?
- Who has prepared a city with streets of gold for us to walk on for eternity?
- Who will be with us in heaven forever?

At one point in my life, I was facing some very trying times, which is one of the reasons I came up with title of this last chapter: "We're All Idiots." I was going through some deep waters in my life and really struggling in the spiritual warfare with Satan who is "a liar and the father of lies" (John 8:44), and who "deceives the whole world" (Revelations 12:9). I was facing the battle of my "flesh lusting against the spirit, and the spirit against the flesh" (Galatians 5:17), and God was teaching me some lessons regarding some of the choices I had made and the consequences I was facing. During that time in my life, a friend called me, and as soon as I answered my phone, he said, "Mark, I have a gun in my hand, and I am going to go kill the man my wife has been having sex with for the last five and a half months. When I kill him, then I'm going to kill myself and end all of this. What do you have to say to me?"

I quickly prayed and asked God to help me and give me wisdom. The Holy Spirit laid on my heart the crucifixion of Jesus on the cross, so I told him, "I want you to go stand at the foot of the cross where Jesus is dying and shedding His blood for you. His feet are at your eye level, so look at the nail in His feet and the blood coming out and how He has to push up on that nail to breathe. Look at the nails in His hands and the blood coming out of them. You realize He was severely beaten before He was nailed to the cross. Those Roman soldiers blindfolded Him and then beat Him—which literally means they put all their weight behind a curled fist. So when they hit Jesus, He didn't know it was coming. Can you imagine that? Think about you closing your eyes and let me hit you as hard as I can. Then they whipped Him. Under Jewish law, they were limited to thirty-nine stripes. But under Roman law, there was no limit, so we have no idea how many times they swatted Him with that cat-of-nine-tails and tore the flesh off His body. Look at the crown of thrones on His head and the blood coming out of the holes around His head and dripping off His face. Let His blood drip in your face! Stand there and let it keep splattering on your face!"

Then I asked him: "Do you get the picture? Now listen carefully to what He is saying as He's hanging there on the cross because He loves you and is willing to die for your sin. It was our sin that nailed Him to that cross! As His blood is dripping on your face, listen to what Jesus is saying: 'Father, forgive them, for they don't know what they are doing.' Now, look over at the man you want to kill, point the gun at him, and pull the trigger if you can. If you can do that while you're standing at the foot of the cross with the blood of Jesus dripping in your face, I have no hope for you, and there is nothing else I can say to you to get you to change your mind and your actions. But how can you do that standing at the foot of the cross while the blood of Jesus is dripping in your face? He loves you, my friend. Do you love Him? Are you going to commit murder and then suicide?" He responded in tears, and said, "Mark, I'm looking at Jesus on the cross. I've put the gun down. I can't do what I wanted to do."

The short version is, that man and his wife put their marriage back together, and they are happier than they have been in years. They love each other and are working at building their marriage because they love God and love each other. What's my point? What you just read is an example of *"What God Can Do with an Idiot"* because I'm an idiot, but God used me to help my friend!

If we really don't understand what God wants us to do, we can seek wise counsel or advice from someone who has a good understanding of the Word of God, loves the Lord, and loves people. We need to keep in mind that demonstrating love to God *and* love to people are the two greatest commandments in God's Word! However, sometimes we still neglect those two great commands and don't do either one. Perhaps we just aren't very good at either one, so we need to take some steps of growth because love is a conscious choice; it's not a feeling or an emotion. I heard a statement once that, "The *choice* to love is the *root* of love, and the *feelings* of love are the *fruit* of love." We should also seek counsel from a person who stands firm on the Word of God as their source of truth. This person from whom we would seek counsel doesn't just preach the truth, but the person lives the truth and speaks the truth in love (Ephesians 4:15). That person can help us grow spiritually because he or she is growing spiritually; he or she can help us to obey God's Word because he or she is obeying God's Word; he or she can help us to think and act like Christ because he or she is thinking and acting like Christ; he or she can help us to grow in obedience to God's Word because he or she is growing in obedience to God's Word and is familiar with the process we referred to earlier called progressive sanctification.

Now answer these questions:

- Why would you be an idiot and not love the Lord your God with all your heart, soul, mind, and strength?
- Why would you not demonstrate your love for God by your obedience to His Word?
- Why would you not demonstrate your love for God by your motivation to glorify Him, which means to give the right opinion of Him in everything that you do?
- Are you willing to admit it to the Lord and ask His forgiveness for whatever degree you are an idiot?
- Are you willing to ask forgiveness to anyone else you've sinned against and offended by demonstrating your stupidity?
- Are you willing to seek to restore that relationship so God can be glorified by your humility and not have to discipline you because of your pride and your lack of forgiveness?

Remember this: at the moment of our salvation, our sins are "removed as far as the east is from the west" (Psalm 103:12), and the "blood of Jesus Christ His Son cleanses us from all sin" (1 John 1:7). When God looks upon us as His children, He doesn't see our sin because He said, "When I see the blood, I will pass over you," which means we as Christians will not spend an eternity in hell because our sins are washed away by the blood of Christ. We are forgiven, and we will spend eternity with the One who "loved us and gave Himself for us" (Ephesians 5:2). What are you going to say when you stand face-to-face with Jesus and look at the scars on His hands, on His side, and around His head where the crown of thorns was jammed? Do you think you could say, "Thank You, Jesus! I love You!"

You might be asking, "Okay, what am I supposed to do right now since I've done some stupid things in my life, and I know I'll probably do something stupid in the days ahead?" If you're dealing with your stupidity right now, the answer is simple: *Admit it*! You could say, "Lord, I was an idiot when I did what I did" or "Lord, I was an idiot when I didn't do what I was supposed to do." As many of us know, the first step in solving a problem is to realize you have one! Don't forget 1 John 1:9: "If we confess our sins, He is faithful and righteous to forgive our sins and to cleanse us from all unrighteousness." Remember, "confess" means to say the same thing God would say about it. We need to remind our stupid selves of what that wise man named Solomon (who also made some stupid choices), wrote in Proverbs 29:23: "A man's pride will bring him low, but a humble spirit will obtain honor."

We should humble ourselves and say, "Lord, I'm proud, and I'm an idiot, but I want to be more like a wise person who follows Your instructions and less like an idiot who thinks he or she knows everything. I want to think like Christ so I can make choices like Christ to be humble, to love You, and to love others like You love us so I don't sin against them or offend them, and to love others no matter how they treat me or respond to me. I want to be a servant like Christ, to bring glory to Your name, to think of You and not myself, and to desire praise from You instead of praise from other people! I also want to think like Christ instead of thinking like Satan who is a "liar and the father of lies" (John 8:44). I want to think like Christ instead of being proud, self-righteous, controlling, stubborn, condescending, unloving, unkind, sinfully angry, and judgmental. We both know that Satan wants to rob You of all the glory he possibly can and bring glory to himself. That liar and father of lies wants me to bring glory to myself instead of You, but I don't want to listen to that liar and deceiver. I want to love You and show my love for You by obeying Your Word and loving others like You love us! Lord, I think I can honestly say the same thing that Agar said when the Holy Spirit inspired him to write Proverbs 30:2–3: "Surely I am more stupid than any man, and I do not have the understanding of a man. Neither have learned wisdom, nor do I have the knowledge of the Holy One.'"

We need to keep in mind that Agar is saying he is not smart like the Holy One is. Agar knows God because he has a relationship with God, and so do you, if you are a Christian. But nobody has the knowledge that the Holy One has because, theologically, God is perfectly smart and knows everything. He is omniscient, which means "all-knowing." We don't have the data in our brains like God has in His. God even told us, "I know the things that come into your mind, every one of them" (Ezekiel 11:5 KJV). Matthew wrote about the knowledge of Jesus: "Jesus knowing their thoughts said, 'Why are you thinking evil in your hearts?'" (Matthew 9:4). Jesus knows when we are thinking right and when we are thinking like idiots!

If we want to know how much of an idiot we truly are, then we need to compare ourselves with God's character—not with the character of another idiot. We need to follow what Paul wrote: "For we dare not make ourselves of the number, or compare ourselves with some that commend themselves: but they measuring themselves by themselves, and comparing themselves among themselves, are not wise" (2 Corinthians 10:12 KJV).

If you want to avoid being more of an idiot than you already are, then don't listen to people who brag on themselves or who constantly try to focus on what they have accomplished or the results of their lives or efforts. Instead, we need to be, "Fixing our eyes on Jesus, the author and finisher of our faith, who *for* the joy set before Him, endured the cross, despising the shame, and is set down at the right hand of the Throne of God" (Hebrews 12:2).

The Greek word *for* in this verse could be literally translated as *instead of*. Jesus didn't do what He did "for the joy" He was going to receive, but He did it because He was willing to sacrifice all the joy that was set before Him. In other words, He sacrificed all the joy of heaven He was experiencing so He could die on the cross Think about Jesus experiencing the joy of being in heaven with God the Father and God the Holy Spirit, along with the angels and the Old Testament people who were in heaven with Him. Then because "God so loved the world that He gave His only begotten Son" (John 3:16), Jesus left the glories of heaven to come to the earth to endure the cross and despise the shame and be raised from the dead so He could offer us eternal life. Jesus did what He did because He loves us. What are we doing to show our love for Him?

God told us in John 14:15, "If you love Me, you will keep My commandments." God wants us to share His Word with those who do not know Jesus as their Lord and Savior. When was the last time you shared the gospel with someone who is not a Christian? Are you looking for ways and opportunities to communicate the death, burial, and resurrection of our Lord and Savior, Jesus Christ? Even though we are not perfect and sometimes we will sin, disobey God's Word, and make wrong choices like idiots, God still wants to use us to be His ambassadors to proclaim the truth to others because we love the Lord and we love people, like Jesus did, and ultimately like John, the Beloved Apostle did, even though he was an idiot sometimes.

From one idiot to another, I want to remind you of what God the

Father said about His Son, Jesus: "This is My beloved Son *in whom I am well pleased*" (Matthew 17:5). If we will think and act like Jesus, His beloved Son, then God can be glorified. Keep in mind to glorify God means to give the right opinion of God. Our lives, our actions, our words, our responses, our attitudes, our motives, our thoughts, our decisions, and all we do, think, or say should give glory to God. Let's go stand at the foot of the cross and look at Jesus. Let's allow His blood to drip in our faces as we listen to what He says. Let's remember that when He returns or takes us home to heaven, that "we will be like Him, because we will see Him just as He is" (1 John 3:2). That's when we will no longer be idiots because the curse of sin will be removed, and we will be given glorified bodies. *Praise the Lord*!

But remember, no matter how big of an idiot you are, God still wants to work in your heart to bring glory to Him by helping you "put off the old man" and "put on the new man" and conform you more to the image of His dear Son, Jesus. Please read carefully the words to the song by Daniel Gennaro, "He's Not Finished with Me Yet." You should be encouraged and thankful for the powerful message of this song and walk away with hope that God is working in your heart to bring glory to Him. You can say to your family, your church, your brother or sister in Christ, or a friend (maybe even one who is not a Christian but could become Christian if you share the gospel with that person) that God loves you, and you love God. You can say with confidence, "Even though I'm an idiot, *'He's not finished with me yet.'*"

I would also strongly encourage you to listen to the encouraging song by Stephen Curtis Chapman entitled "Something Beautiful." This wonderful song clearly communicates the fact that no matter what you're facing in your life, no matter how difficult the pathway is that you are walking, or even if you've made some stupid choices and revealed that fact you are an idiot, God is able to take that situation and turn it into "Something Beautiful."

This song greatly encourages us and motivates us to "run with endurance the race that is set before us, fixing our eyes on Jesus, the author and perfecter of faith" (Hebrews 12:1–2). Even though you might be going through some deep waters and trials of your faith, remember, God is able to take all the horrible things you've been going through and turn all that into "Something Beautiful." He can do it because He is all powerful, all-knowing, present everywhere, perfectly sinless, gracious, merciful, patient, and loving. As you listen to this song, think about what God can do in your life. It's not what He *will* do (that decision is up to Him), but it's what He *can* do if He wants to do it! Trust Him because He's perfect. He doesn't make mistakes, and He loves you. Think about and mediate on Ephesians 3:20: "Now to Him who is able to do far more abundantly beyond all that we ask or think, according to the power that works within us, to Him be glory in the church and in Christ Jesus to all generations forever and ever, Amen." God has the power and the wisdom to take any situation and turn it into "Something Beautiful" that can encourage any of us as an idiot no matter how stupid we've been.

There is one final song that communicates this whole process of *What God Can Do with an Idiot*. I would encourage you to listen another song by Stephen Curtis Chapman entitled, "A Glorious Unfolding." Listen to the song online and memorize the words because they communicate a powerful message to anybody who is going through some deep waters, or trials of faith, or even the consequences for being an idiot because he or she didn't obey God's Word. No matter what you are experiencing or how difficult it is, it's going to be "A Glorious Unfolding" from God's perspective for you or someone you know or love.

Remember, my friend (and hopefully my brother or sister in Christ), that God "is able to do exceedingly abundantly above all that we could ask or think" even with a couple of idiots like you and me and the other idiots we know! Praise the Lord that He's not finished with us yet, and He can take our lives and turn them into something beautiful that will bring glory to His name! We need to remember that we are in a process, and God is in control. Our situation can be a glorious unfolding. Keep in mind and memorize this verse: "And we know that God causes all things to work together for good to those who love God, to those who are called according to His purpose" (Romans 8:28). God didn't say "some things." He said, *"all things."* He didn't say, "All things are good." He said, "All things *work together* for good." I hope we get to heaven soon so when we see each other, we can smile and say, "Remember what God did with an idiot?" If we don't remember, God will remember! I wonder if David, Peter, or Paul will say to me, "Mark, I thought I was the only idiot till I watched your life, and then I realized, like you said, 'We're all idiots!'"

So from one idiot to another, let's be humble and admit "We're All Idiots" and ask God to help us spend time in His Word, spend time in prayer, keep growing in thinking and acting like Christ, faithfully attend a church, and generously give to advance the cause of Christ in our communities and around the world.

We need to ask God to help us use the gifts and abilities He gave us to be servants and to bring glory to His name (not ours). We need to ask God to help us share the gospel with people who don't know Jesus as their Lord and Savior. We need to ask God to help us encourage our brothers and sisters in Christ who have sinned, or are currently sinning, to admit they are idiots (after you admit you are an idiot) and to repent from their sin. We need to encourage them and help them to change and grow to think and act more like Christ, the One who loved us, and gave Himself for us!

We need to show the love we have for the Lord, and the love we have for people—not only groups of people, but individuals. We can't just focus on groups of people or large crowds. We also need to focus on individuals who are hurting or struggling in their life, or in their marriage or family, or in the job or ministry. If you're not willing to sit down and talk with an idiot, then you just proved you're an idiot. Think about how Jesus responded to those who offended him to the point of 'denying Him' and 'forsaking

Him' at the most critical time in His life. Don't just think about results in your life or ministry, think about relationships and demonstrating godly love to others like Jesus did, and allow people to see the evidence in your life regarding *What God Can Do with an Idiot!*

CPSIA information can be obtained
at www.ICGtesting.com
Printed in the USA
LVOW08s0715231116
514078LV00001B/2/P